'20

A BEAUTIFUL, GLORIOUS SHE

Women's Role in the Godhead

Eulalie Hendricks

ISBN 978-1-64140-730-4 (paperback)
ISBN 978-1-64140-731-1 (digital)

Christian Faith Publishing, Inc.
832 Park Avenue
Meadville, PA 16335
www.christianfaithpublishing.com

Printed in the United States of America

Contents

Acknowledgments

I want to thank Joseph Prince and his ministry for opening my eyes to the gospel of grace. For over forty years, I lived under the ministry of the law, which brought shame, guilt, condemnation, and death. For over forty years, I was blinded to who I am in Christ Jesus and to all that is mine, thanks to the finished work of the cross. Thanks to Joseph Prince, the veil of the law has been stripped from my eyes, and I have stepped into His marvelous grace. Whereas once I was blind, now I see. I see the depths of His glorious love for me, and I know beyond know that I am deeply loved, highly favored, and greatly blessed. I would encourage every Christian to order Joseph Prince's resources, at www.josephprinceonline.com, to learn all that you are and all that you have in Christ Jesus.

My hope is that other women will not spend the majority of their Christian lives robbed of the joy, the power, and the blessings that are already theirs in Christ Jesus. My desire is to tear down the veil of the law that has kept so many of us blinded and to reveal who we really are in Christ Jesus. My prayer is that women will unleash their Sarah blessing and learn to walk in the renewal of their health, youth, and beauty; that they will release their Abraham blessing and learn to walk in the fullness of financial provision and prosperity; and that they will apprehend the awesomeness of their identity in the Godhead, and learn to walk in the "heart" knowledge that we were created to be His heavenly princesses, His glorious shekinahs.

I also want to thank my family. I come from a heritage of godly Christian men and women on both sides. Each blessed relative has left a profound impact on my life and has a huge part to play in who I am. I have been so very blessed to have the love, affection, and acceptance of hundreds of relatives, and I am so very proud to call each and every one of you my family. Thank you for your steadfast, Christlike love toward me and for always heartily receiving me into your warm, generous hearts and your gracious, loving arms. I am so blessed in my family!

The Holy Spirit:
A Beautiful, Glorious She

For months, I had asked the Lord to show me how the Holy Spirit, who God calls "the Comforter or Helper" (John 14:16, 26) relates to us as women, whom God calls "comforters or helpers" (Gen. 2:18, 20). Daily I asked Him for wisdom and insight regarding the significance of using the same word (in Hebrew *azar*; in Greek *boethos*) for both of us. One morning during my devotions, I was again pondering and querying when I distinctly heard, "The Holy Spirit is a beautiful, glorious She."

After my initial thoughts of "Wow! Really? Wouldn't that truly be so amazing?"

I responded, "Wow! Lord, this would make such perfect sense—that our Comforter/Helper is a She! Why wouldn't woman be represented in the Godhead? If both male and female are created in His image, then shouldn't we be seen and represented as well? If God calls both women and the Holy Spirit by the same name, wouldn't this mean that we were made in the image of the Holy Spirit? What an amazing thought and revelation! Is it true, Lord? Is this really from You? Is the Holy Spirit a beautiful, glorious She?"

If this were true, this would essentially mean that a man and a woman, together with the Lord, truly constitute a three-strand cord, a trinity—Jesus-husband-wife, like Father-Son-Holy Spirit—that we are an equal part of the Trinity, a three-fold cord that cannot be easily broken. Men and women would be equal partners with different but equal strengths and powers. We would not be subservient, as we have been taught in our churches, but would have equal standing and status in the eyes of God. Are we the feminine, nurturing, relational, sensitive side of God as represented and characterized by the Holy Spirit?

God did not think it good for man to be alone, so He created for him a comforter/helper (Gen. 2:18, 20); and Jesus did not want to leave His bride, the church, alone after He had ascended, so He sent to us a Comforter/Helper (John 14:16, 26).

This would mean that women are not an afterthought or second-rate citizens. We were part of the plan from the beginning. We were represented in the Godhead from the beginning. What a powerful thought to think that we are modeled after an essential part of the Godhead! We are the relational, nurturing, sensitive side of God. We are His beauty and His grace personified.

We were not brought forth from the dust of the earth like every other created creature. They came from baser substances, whereas we were brought forth from a living, breathing, created being, from a place near to the heart of man, and then we were fashioned by the hands of God. We were the only beings created in this fashion. Does not our origin alone speak to something more refined and special? We were not fashioned from earth but from things above.

Our nature testifies that we yearn to live close to the heart, close to our husband's heart, and close to our Heavenly Father's heart. It is our nature to live above baser things, above all that is crass and cruel about the world. Our dreams are full of happily ever after, sweetness, and light. Our souls were designed for gentleness, purity, relationship, and hope. Like the Holy Spirit, it is our nature to nurture—to soothe, to comfort, to encourage, to support, and to believe the best of those we love. We compliment man and complete him. Men keep our world protected and safe, and we make the world beautiful and full of grace.

We are not lesser beings with a lesser role to play. On the contrary, we were the pinnacle of God's creation and we play the greater role. We are the ones who bring forth new life. We are the ones who nurtured and bore the Savior. God didn't use a man's help to bring his Son into the world; He used a woman. He trusted a woman to carry and nurture His beloved Son. He would not have had to use a woman, for He is God; yet He chose to use a woman—to use half of a woman's DNA to bring forth our Savior. Does this not reveal a whole lot about how much God esteems our sex?

Once Jesus was grown, He surrounded Himself with women. We helped support His ministry, and we encouraged and loved Him while He walked on this earth (Luke 8:2–3). We were invited to serve a vital role in His ministry. Isn't it funny how Jesus never said that we should be seen but not heard? Isn't it interesting that some of His most intimate relationships were with women? Jesus esteemed and treasured us and held us very dear, despite growing up in a very patriarchal society. It may have rankled some of the men of that day that Jesus gave women so much of His time, attention, and honor. Isn't it also interesting that one of the gospels that did not endure through time was Mary Magdalene's? As a woman, I would have loved to hear her account of Jesus's life; to hear the story from a woman's perspective.

Fred P. Miller writes in his book, *Zechariah and Jewish Renewal,* that "the Shekinah" in Hebrew is a feminine noun. The "glory of the Lord," commonly called the Shekinah in Hebrew, is feminine. He writes, "The word "Shekinah," itself is not in the biblical text but the concept,… clearly is. The word most certainly is derived from "shakan," and whoever first used the word "Shekinah" coined it as a substantive (noun form) from the verbal forms used to describe the "abiding, dwelling, or habitation" of the physical manifestations of God described in Ex 24:16; Ex. 40:35; Nu. 9:16-18, and numerous other places where "shakan" is used."

The word is also used to describe the mystical Shekinah presence in the tabernacle. It was the light that shone above the mercy seat of the ark of the covenant, the divine radiance that dwelt between the wings of the cherubim in the holy of holies. The word *mishkan* is often translated as "tabernacle." Mishkan means "dwelling place of She who dwells," or Shekinah.

Miller continues,

> It is interesting that Isaiah refers to the Shekinah using feminine pronouns. Especially in Isaiah 51. Particularly, in Isaiah 51:9 & 10 and its context, the pronouns are feminine. In verse 10, the KJV uses "thou" and "it" to refer to the Shekinah. Both pronouns are feminine in the Hebrew. The Qumran text makes the feminine form certain by adding a yod to 2fs. Literally, feminine 'you she' is translated in KJV "thou it."[1]

He further explains that whatever noun one calls it, such physical representations of the "presence" are in the Bible. What did Ezekiel see leave the temple (Ezek. 10:19; 11:23)? It is certain that whatever name you call the "presence," it is linked with the fiery cloud at Sinai. Hebrews scholars have chosen to use the name Shekinah to name the Biblically described mystical thing "dwelling" or "abiding."

The Shekinah is now manifested as She indwells Her people as Spirit. Miller states that Isaiah 57:15 says as much, "For thus says the high and lofty One who inhabits ('shakan') eternity, whose name is Holy; I dwell ('shakan') in the high and holy place, and with him also that is of a contrite and humble spirit, to revive the spirit of the humble, and to revive the heart of the contrite ones."

Miller concludes that the word *shokeyn*, translated "who inhabits" in this passage, is as close to the meaning and direct use of the word Shekinah as one will find. According to this verse, Shekinah is the She who inhabits heaven and human hearts at one and the same time.

This provokes in me other questions: Why have we never been told this in four thousand years of biblical history? How can I have

---

[1] Ibid.

been saved for over forty years, yet never have read about this or made this connection? Even after reading *The Shack*, by William Young, I did not seriously give thought to the Holy Spirit being a She, like Sarayu, any more than I thought God would be a fluffy big-hearted black woman, as delightful as that would be. I just didn't make that leap, or seriously consider that there could be anything real about Young's characterizations. Although intriguing, I dismissed it as fantasy and too farfetched.

I believe the reason we have been kept in the dark is because Satan works extra hard to keep women blinded to the truth of who we are in Christ, and to our role in the Godhead. After the fall, God said, "I am declaring war between you (Satan) and the Woman, between your offspring and hers. He (Jesus) will wound your head; you (Satan) will wound his (Jesus') heel" (Gen. 3:14, 15, MSG). God declared a state of war between women and Satan; therefore, Satan hates us with every fiber of his being. He knows that we would be the one who bore the Savior, and he knows that Jesus is going to crush his head. Once Jesus showed up, Satan's days were numbered.

Why is it war? It is the age-old battle between darkness and light. Satan is darkness and Shekinah is light. Satan is the force of wickedness, evil, sickness, and death on our planet, whereas Shekinah is the force of goodness, holiness, healing, and life. Satan hates everything we were created to be, so he works overtime to try and steal, kill, and destroy us (John 10:10). Like a roaring lion, he roams about spewing lies and accusations, trying to steal our knowledge of who we are in Christ, trying to beat us down and kill us with abuse, trying to steal from us our dignity, our value, our worth, our identity, and, ultimately, our joy (1 Pet.5:8).

There is a marvelous new trilogy out called *Up from the Ashes* by Pastor Ron Leedy, which aptly describes Satan's evil machinations against women. Leedy relates so many of the struggles and ugly mindsets that women have had to endure, even unto the present time, when they are viewed by ungodly men as nothing but sex objects, pieces of meat, and just a set of boobs. During an end-time period of chaos, Leedy reveals through his characters how evil man can be apart from God, and how loving and righteous man is with God. It is a story I couldn't put down, and I love that Leedy portrays strong, capable, independent, courageous women and children who help the men triumph over evil.

In the book, the Christian survivors, the homesteaders, create a godly community based on appreciation, respect, and interdependency for each person's unique strengths and talents, gleaning from each other without regard for age, race, or sex in order to survive and protect what they have built. It is a suspenseful, futuristic, well-told tale that descriptively redefines the age-old war of good against evil, particularly where women are concerned.

If Satan can keep us abused, defeated, depressed, and in the dark, then he wins. *But* we have the glory of the LORD on our side, and She is chasing away all the ugly darkness and deception, and we are walking into the truth of Her glorious light; we are apprehending the fullest manifestation of our Shekinah identity. It is so refreshing to see others, like the author Pastor Leedy, who sees and understands all that we were meant to be as women, and exalts us to our rightful position as helpmeets and comforters, crediting us with all the strengths, power, and abilities we are capable of, and giving to the world an example of women functioning at their full potential as His shekinahs. Truly, such glory-filled writing gladdens my heart!

Jesus's death and resurrection secured for us victory over Satan. Jesus elevated us to the position of sons and daughters of the Most High, adopting us as blood-bought heirs who will reign with Him forever (Gal. 3:29; Rom. 4:14-17). Satan knows that soon woman's offspring, Jesus, will come down on his head with both feet and stomp him into the dirt (Rom. 16:20). Satan also knows that once his blinders are lifted from women's eyes and we start apprehending the fullest manifestation of all that is ours as His shekinahs, then we will light up the world!

Notice Satan did not try to con Adam, but he came to Eve. It should also be noted that when God gave the commandment to

Adam to not eat of the tree of knowledge of good and evil, Eve had not yet been created. The commandment was given to Adam, not to Eve, so we might presume that because she received the information secondhand, perhaps she didn't fully realize the import of God's words.

Satan knows that our natures are innocent, gullible, and naïve, and he takes full advantage of that at every turn. It has always been his mission and handiwork to keep us beaten down, treated like chattel, and, tragically too often, despicably and treacherously abused in the most disgusting ways imaginable. Ceaselessly he carries out his war against women and their children. Satan's relentless brutal assaults are meant to annihilate and destroy the comforters, to delude and disable the shekinahs.

Satan preys on women and children and he sees our demise as the easiest way to bruise and insult the Godhead and to incapacitate and weaken humanity. Like the pillar of cloud by day and the pillar of fire by night, we shelter, we guide, we protect, we nurture, and we teach our families, keeping them ever mindful, sensitive, and close to the heart of God (Ex. 13: 21). Look what happened to the Israelites once the Shekinah Glory left the tabernacle—they were scattered to the four winds. Ladies, we are the shekinah glory to our families and to the world.

We are the comforters and the helpers on our planet. Often, we are the ones who keep our families on the right path. We are the ones who train our children in the paths of righteousness. We are the ones who take up the shield of faith when Satan's fiery darts threaten our families. We are the ones who sustain our families with nutritional food and keep them well clothed. We are the ones who make our homes a warm, loving, peaceful place that fosters spiritual, emotional, and physical growth. We are the main helpers, the worker bees, who keep our churches healthy, strong, and functioning. We are the force for love, compassion, and healing on our planet. We are the shekinahs for our families and the world.

It is time for us to rise up, O daughters of the Most High, and to walk in the power, and the glory of who God created us to be. It is time to revel in our position in the Godhead. He modeled us after the ineffable, ministering side of Himself, and He empowers us with an immeasurable ability to love.

How many times have we met women who love a man who by all outward appearance seems very undeserving? Yet, obviously, the wife sees things in her husband that others do not. She has the ability to see the good and to focus on those qualities, the same way the Holy Spirit only sees Jesus in us, not our failings and shortcomings. Have we not seen this kind of love manifested in wives and mothers all over the world—women who doggedly hang in there with their wayward, troubled, wounded loved ones, refusing to give up on them? That is the amazing power of grace and love that is part of our gifting as women. We do not give up easily because our Heavenly Father never gives up on us.

It does not matter how badly we fail; we have the full assurance that our Father in Heaven will never leave us nor forsake us. Like the Holy Spirit, women are built for grace. It is ingrained into the very core of our being. That is why you can see women who are abused and treated despicably by their husbands supernaturally endure year after year. To others looking on, it seems impossible, unbearable, and unsustainable, yet against all understanding, these women persevere. We endeavor to believe the best until it is just impossible to do so.

Yet we are not God, so some of us who gave it their utmost have failed. I do not believe any Christian woman gives up on an ungodly husband without giving it her uttermost best effort. Unlike our Heavenly Father, we are human, and each of us has a limit to what we can endure. We are all daughters of Sarah (1 Pet. 3:6), His princesses, but it is inevitable that some of us are going to get yoked to immature, selfish, unkind men. When that happens, some of us will be able to lead our husbands to the Lord and into a more understanding way of dwelling with us, and some of us will not.

A Christian counselor once told me, "Some people are easier to love from afar." As a comforter and nurturer, it is your job to keep you and your children safe. If you have tried counseling, and you have exhausted every avenue you know in order to seek help for your husband, then I would encourage you to do what is necessary to keep you and your family safe. After the Israelites turned their back on God over and over again and kept whoring after other gods, the Shekinah finally left the tabernacle.

If a husband refuses to get help and continues to deal treacherously with his wife and children, then his shekinah, his princess, should depart. At this juncture, the husband has two choices—one, he will decide he treasures his wife and family and he will be willing to seek help; or two, he says, "Good riddance!" and he sets off to find another woman he can abuse. If the husband will seek help, then the wife may have every hope of reconciliation. If the husband walks away, then he was not worthy of his wife's love and affection. As Jesus instructed the disciples in Luke 9:5, sometimes your only recourse is to shake the dust from your feet and move on.

This woman needs to cling to the truth that God takes what man means for evil against us and He turns it to our good (Rom. 8:28). He is a rewarder of those who diligently seek Him (Heb. 11:6). And "No weapon formed against you shall prosper, and every tongue which rises against you in judgement you shall condemn. This is the heritage of the servants of the LORD, and their righteousness is from Me, says the LORD" (Isa. 54:17). We are the righteousness of our God in Christ (2 Cor. 5:21).

We are made righteous thanks to the finished work of Christ. When God looks at us, even those of us who have failed in our marriages, He only sees us through the lens of the cross. God the Father doesn't see all the ways we have failed; He only sees us through the righteous robes of our Savior. His promise to us is, "For I will be merciful to their unrighteousness, and their sins and their lawless deeds I will remember no more" (Heb. 8:12). We have His assurance, "Therefore, there is now no condemnation for those who are in Christ Jesus" (Rom. 8:1).

Jesus paid the penalty in His own body for every sin we have ever committed, or will ever commit in the future. That is why He could say "It is finished" (John 19:30). The woman who has lost can take comfort in the fact that God will restore unto her all the years the locusts have eaten (Joel 2:25), He will restore double for our troubles (Zech. 9:12), and when God restores it is better than before (Job 42:12–16). So take heart and rejoice, O you shekinahs, O you daughters of the Most High (Gal 4:4–7), because you are His heavenly princess (1 Pet. 3:6), you are His royal priestess (1 Pet. 2:9), you are His queen-priestess (Rev. 1:5, 6), and you are deeply loved (1 John 4:16–19), highly favored (Eph. 2:4-8), and greatly blessed! (Prov. 10:6)

We are His beautiful shekinahs. We were created to be comforters, helpers, healers, and ministers of His grace. We are called to be a soothing balm on the angry wound of this planet, to impart His radiance of goodness, healing, and love, and to shine His light of grace in the darkness of our fallen world. Every person grows up amidst our fallen humanity, so we all have wounds. God designed women to be sensitive and relational so that we have the insight and ability to administer comfort and healing to the brokenhearted. Like Jesus, God gave us the grace and power to heal the sick, feed and clothe the poor, comfort the bereaved and broken, and to speak life into the wounded and deceived.

Like the Holy Spirit, He has given His shekinahs all His ministering gifts—words of wisdom, words of knowledge, faith, gifts of healing, words of prophecy, words of exhortation, works of miracles, gift of tongues, interpretation of tongues, acts of service, administrations, gift of evangelism, gift of teaching, and the gift of preaching (1 Cor. 12). The Holy Spirit, our Shekinah Glory that indwells us, gives us the power to perform and accomplish all God's ministering gifts.

We are the power for healing, for comfort, and for ministering on our planet, but we are a force that remains to be seen. What would our world look like if each one of His glorious shekinahs rose up and began walking in the fullness of His resurrected life and power? Would we not be a light to be reckoned with? If every shekinah unleased her light on this planet, would not our brilliance overwhelm the kingdom of darkness and usher in revival as the world has never known? As God reveals to us the full identity of who we are in Jesus and the fullness of who we are in the Godhead, I pray His grace, His glory, His presence, and His power will be unleashed in miracle proportions in the lives of each and every one of us. Using the words of the prophet Isaiah, God encourages all His blessed shekinahs to "arise and shine, for your light is come! It's come! Arise and shine, for your light is come! And the glory of the Lord is risen upon you, so arise and shine!" (Isa. 60:1)

Revelation

Once, as a woman, I felt like a biblical afterthought, a second-rate citizen, but now I know that I was created equal in standing and status as men with different but equal strengths and gifting and that I am modeled after the feminine side of God, His Holy Spirit.

Prayer of Praise

Thank You, Jesus, that Your glory shines within me. I receive, O Lord, that I am made in the image of Your Holy Spirit and that I was in your thoughts from the very beginning. Thank You, Lord, that I am created unique with an especial purpose to be a force for Your gentleness, goodness, healing, and peace on this planet. Thank You, Jesus, that You created me from a living breathing created being and drew me from a place close to the heart. Help me to be ever mindful to live close to Your heart, close to my husband's heart, and close to the hearts of others. Help me to sense and feel when comfort, love, and help is needed and make me an instrument of Your healing. Teach me, O Lord, how to walk in the fullness of my special calling

My Revelation: Unveiled and Unleashed

I was fifty-five years old. I was unemployed for four years running. I was twice divorced and shunned by most of my Christian friends. I had my whole world yanked out from underneath me twice. I lost two homes and two horse places that I had worked like a dog to build. I lost two lives, two worlds, and two church families. I had lost my mother two years prior and two brothers before that. As a teenager, I lost my *Mary Poppins* father to divorce, drugs, and alcohol. Loss, loss, and more loss! Life seemed to be nothing but horrific loss!

I was distraught, devastated, discouraged, and depressed. I was confused in my faith, and so weary of the struggle to survive. I felt without hope, thoroughly exhausted, and on the verge of an emotional and mental collapse. I was angry at God because I believed He was angry and disgusted with me. I felt I was nothing but a huge disappointment to Him, and that when He looked at me, all He would see was a big *F* branded on my forehead for "failure".

With God, I felt condemned as a Christian before I was even out of the chute—molested young and promiscuous in my teens—I just knew God was waiting up in His heaven with His giant flyswatter, and at any moment, He was going to squash me flat like a bug, because that is what I deserved. I believed He hated me and that He was trying to snuff me out, to suffocate me, by dishing out overwhelming trials—that I had been weighed in the balance and found wanting. I felt I could never measure up. I could never undo my mistakes—that I was completely and utterly without hope. I was judged! I was guilty! I was condemned! *And then came grace!*

Grace lifted the veil of the law, which brings guilt, shame, condemnation, and death. Grace came and ushered in the new covenant, which brings His righteousness, health, provision, shalom peace, and life. Grace came and unleashed my Abraham blessing, my Sarah blessing, all in Benjamin-generation blessing proportions. The veil of the law fell from my eyes, and I could see that it is God's heart and His greatest pleasure to pour out on me, and in me His pure, unadulterated grace of undeserved, unearned, and unmerited favor. Grace came and unveiled a lifetime of deception and unleashed a torrential flood of blessing. My revelation was this:

- That once as a woman I felt like a biblical afterthought, a second rate citizen, but now I know that I was created equal in standing and status as men, with different but equal strengths and gifting, and that I am modeled after the feminine side of God, His Holy Spirit;
- That once I was lost, but now I am found;
- That once I didn't see how Bible stories were relevant, but now I know that every type, shadow, similitude, and faith picture reveals something about my Heavenly Father's love for me;
- That once I was blind, but now I see;
- That once I felt my heart would explode under the strain of troubles and trials, but now I feel as though my heart will burst with joy and gratitude;
- That once I walked in shame, guilt, and condemnation, but now I walk in His unearned, undeserved, unbridled favor and blessing;
- That once I believed I deserved disease, depression, punishment, and judgment, but now I know that thanks to Christ's finished work on the cross, I don't get what I deserve—I get what Jesus deserves;

- That once I lived in constant fear of His wrath and displeasure, but now I know that I am saved from fear, wrath, death, and hell, and I am saved unto His safety, His shalom peace, His love, and every blessing the Father desires to lavish on His Son;
- That once I was harsh and critical with my words because I felt God was harsh and critical of me, but now I know that I am the righteousness of God in Christ and my words have creative power, therefore I choose to speak life;
- That once I believed God was against me, but now I know that He is irrevocably for me;
- That once I believed my obligation was to love God with all my heart, soul, and mind (which I continually failed at), but now I know that herein is love, not that we love Him, but that He loved us;
- That once I believed Jesus's miracle manifestations were for another people during another time, but now I know Jesus is the same yesterday, today, and forever, and every promise is for me;
- That once I saw myself as disgusting and wretched in His sight, but now I know that I am His heavenly princess, His royal priestess, and His most beloved daughter;
- That once I believed I was overlooked and unworthy, but now I know that I am the seed of Abraham through faith, an heir according to the promise, and as a blood-bought heir, I inherit all the blessings of Abraham, all the blessings of Sarah, which means God will supernaturally renew, restore, protect, and provide for me all my days;
- That once I felt like such a failure, but now I know I am an outrageous success, that He blesses all the works of my hands and He makes all my gifts precious stones that prosper me;
- That once I believed Jesus forgave other people's sins, but that mine were too offensive, but now I know that thinking

was blindness and pride, that Jesus was beaten to a bloody, unrecognizable pulp to pay for *my* sins, therefore, I am completely and utterly forgiven;

- That once I believed I was less than pond scum in the eyes of God, but now I know that was the *big lie*. I am precious in His sight and His thoughts toward me are only precious;
- That once I felt powerless and insignificant, but now I know I am His beloved shekinah and I am fearsome in His glory and majesty; and
- That once I believed as a woman that I didn't matter much to God, but now I know that I am His precious shekinah, that I was modeled after the Holy Spirit, and that I was a part of the plan and part of the Godhead from the beginning.

This was my revelation—that grace came in the person of Jesus Christ. Under the new covenant, Jesus came and met all the requirements of the law on my behalf, so that now I don't get what I deserve, I get what Jesus deserves. "Amazing Grace, how sweet the sound that saved a wretch like me. I once was lost, but now am found; was blind, but now I see."

The veil represents the law and the law brings blindness and death, as in three thousand souls perished at Mt. Sinai when Moses gave the law. "The letter (the law) kills, but the Spirit gives life" (2 Cor. 3:6). When Christ died, the veil of the law in the temple was rent in two because Jesus kept the law perfectly on our behalf and paid the full penalty for the law's demand for us in His own body. Now there is nothing standing in the way between us and our Heavenly Father. Jesus tore the veil so that we can come boldly before the Father without shame and condemnation. The law's demands have been met, thanks to Jesus, so there is no longer a need for the veil.

The Son of God offered His body as ransom to be scourged and pierced, offering His own Holy blood to cut a new covenant with the God the Father in order to redeem us from death and the curse. He laid down His life to usher in His new covenant of amazing Grace.

Christ has taken away the veil of the law between us and God so that now we can come boldly into the throne of grace as blood-bought sons and daughters of the Most High. Through Christ's finished work on the cross we have been fully restored as blood-bought heirs, which entitle us to every blessing of God.

Grace came in the person of Jesus Christ. Through Christ's death and resurrection, we have access to His glorious gift of salvation. We are completely and thoroughly redeemed from death and hell, and we are saved unto every good and perfect gift from our Heavenly Father's hand. Jesus secured for us a complete pardon and won for us His right to every blessing of God. Therefore, we are not only saved *from* everything we deserve, we are saved *unto* everything Jesus deserves. He performed for us a divine exchange—He took the penalty of our sins and gave us the rewards of His righteousness. Now we are called "the righteousness of God in Christ" (2 Cor. 5:21).

Through the gift of our Comforter, the Holy Spirit, the glory of the Lord has returned to our planet, and She radiates in the lives of all those who have invited Jesus into their hearts. Jesus came so that none should perish, but that all should come to the saving knowledge of His Grace, and He left for us our Shekinah, our Comforter, our Helper—His Glory. Jesus infuses us with His power, His presence, His glory, and His grace, and He indwells us; He intimately abides with all those who belong to Him. Jesus has given us His Glory and He has made us one with Himself and the Father (John 17:21-23). God's Glory has been restored to us.

Jesus unveiled for me His glorious grace, and in the blink of an eye, He lifted me from wretched-sinner status to precious-princess status. I felt like Job, when he said, "I have heard of You by the hearing of the ear, but now my eye sees you" (Job 42:5). It is a funny thing about darkness; it cannot exist in the presence of even the smallest flicker of light. The merest light chases it away. Once I caught just a glimmer of truth about grace, a whole lifetime of lies, deceit, and darkness were exposed, like a whole football stadium of LED floodlights were flashed directly at them. For the first time in my Christian walk, I felt free. Grace and truth chased away the darkness and the truth of my Heavenly Father's love for me set me free from a lifetime of gross deception (John 8:32).

In the blink of an eye I recognized it wasn't ever God who hated me and sought my demise—it was Satan. He had convinced me that I was despicable in God's sight. He blinded me using the law to accuse me and defeat me. Through the law, he blinded me to God's grace by keeping me self-focused on my failures rather than focused on what Jesus says about me and what He had already done with my failures. No person can live up to God's holy standard. The purpose of the law was to show us that we cannot live a perfect, sinless life, that we are not God, that we will always fall short, and that my best effort is still only filthy rags compared to a holy God. Hence, why God provided for us a new covenant, one based on Jesus's obedience, not mine. Now it is not at all about me, but 100 percent about what Jesus did for me. What a blessed relief! "In this is love, not that we loved God, but that He loved us, and sent His Son to be a propitiation for our sins" (1 John 4:10).

As the Lord unveiled the truth of His great love for me, I learned that Jesus became my High Priest according to the order of Melchizedek. This means Jesus can *only* bless me—He cannot curse me. Some preachers try to teach us that Jesus gives us sickness, diseases, and trials to teach us lessons. There is not a single example of this in the New Testament. Not once did Jesus say, "I am going to teach you a lesson on humility, so here is some leprosy." On the contrary, His ministry was only one of healing and blessing because as our High Priest, He became our righteousness forever. He stands in our place before the Father and He gives us His everlasting righteousness and blessings. We have a perfect High Priest who perfectly blesses.

Once I saw and understood that I am irrevocably blessed, the Lord unleashed His promises of blessings in His word. I began to see verses I never noticed before. I began to see that Jesus qualifies me for every blessing, that every word, every promise, and every faith picture was for me. Why don't we experience miracles? Many of us grow up believing miracles are not for us today. How sad! Jesus's simple explanation is "You have not because you ask not" (James 4:2). He said, "Whatsoever things you ask when you pray, believe that you receive them, and you will have them" (Mark 11:24). Jeremiah prophesied, "Call to Me and I will answer you and show you great and mighty things which you do not know" (Jer. 33:3). Jesus hasn't changed, so who changed? The answer is "Us." We changed.

"I am the Beginning and the End," says the Lord, "Jesus has the final word" (Rev. 1:8), and all that He says He will do (Num. 23:19). Jesus told His disciples, "Wait for the Promise of the Father" (Acts 1:4). What promise you may ask? He continued, "But you shall receive power when the Holy Spirit has come upon you; and you shall be witnesses to Me in Jerusalem...and to the end of the earth" (Acts 1:8). God's word says that when the Holy Spirit comes upon us, we shall receive power. I believe we do not have power because so many of us do not even know that we have been given power. The Holy Spirit—the glory of the Lord—His Shekinah glory indwells us and that indwelling gives us power. We do not walk in that power because we have been so blinded to our identity in Christ.

Through Joseph Prince's ministry, God unleashed in my life all that is mine as a daughter of the Most High. Truly, it was like walking out of a dark prison cell into the glorious light. How refreshing to learn that God will never be angry with me again, that He exhausted all His wrath in the body of His beloved Son, so that He could redeem to Himself a people once and for all! How comforting to know that Jesus has made us accepted and beloved in the Father's eyes, that we have been exalted as blood-bought heirs and blessed with every possible blessing! How amazing to realize that God is on my side, that all the hosts of heaven are on my side, and because I have Jesus, the very universe is on my side! If God is for me, who can stand against me?

It is remarkable that once I was introduced to His Grace, I went from believing I was cursed to knowing I was blessed. Just as soon as

I repented (that means having changed my mind about my thinking) of my attitude (which means I started believing what God says about me), God's favor started to hunt me down. I was working as a substitute teacher at the time, and suddenly parents started calling the teachers lauding my praises. Now I hadn't done anything different, with the exception of agreeing with what God says about me, and suddenly I was finding favor everywhere I went.

Within months of my apprehending and claiming all God's promises and blessings in my life, I was given a total princess assignment. God gave me a job teaching one student for an international business couple at master-teacher wages. What unbelievable favor! A year later, He gave me a publishing contract with a major academic publisher. He gave my children incredibly high-paying jobs. My daughter jumped from $50/hour to $135/hour. The list goes on and on, and all because I began to believe and to speak what God says about me. My revelation was that I am His beautiful blessed shekinah and He delights in blessing me and He takes the greatest pleasure in prospering me. The good news is, so are you!

Revelation
Once I was lost, but now I am found.

Prayer of Praise
Thank You, Jesus, for opening my eyes to Your glorious Grace and for revealing to me my position in the Godhead. Lord, I was once so very blind, lost in deception and lies, but now that I know the truth of who I am in Christ, I can see how deeply I am loved. I know Your favor and blessing is unreservedly mine, and I receive that I am Your blessed shekinah and the most beloved daughter of the Most High. As heir to Your throne of Grace, every blessing is already mine. You hold absolutely nothing back from me and every good and perfect gift that You desire to lavish on Jesus, You now lavish on me. Thank You, Jesus, that You found me, and now I walk in the glorious light of Your immeasurable love.

Faith Pictures: Not Just Stories 'Bout a Bunch of Old Dead Gals

The Bible is a living book. It is filled with stories for our instruction and encouragement. Upon first glance, one may wonder, what could those stories about people who lived so long ago have any have anything to do with me today? Hidden in these stories are all manner of types and shadows that speak to all the generations that will follow. In these stories we learn God's heart toward His people. With every interaction that He has had with man, God communicates something about Himself. Through His words, through His promises, through His prophets, and through a variety of faith pictures, God reveals to us His heart of love toward us. Tucked within these stories are love letters from our Heavenly Father that still bless us today.

We are living in a prophetic time. God is revealing His wisdom and truths which are manifested through His words that were spoken hundreds, even thousands of years ago. Gifted teachers have the ability to take what was said long ago and make it relevant for our lives today. Anointed teaching helps us to grow in wisdom so that we can live our lives from a position of victory instead of defeat. God encourages us to get wisdom. In Ephesians 1:17–19, it says,

> That the God of our Lord Jesus Christ, the Father of glory, may give to you the spirit of wisdom and revelation in the knowledge of Him, the eyes of your understanding being enlightened; that you may know what is the hope of His calling, what

are the riches of the glory of His inheritance in the saints, and what is the exceeding greatness of His power toward us who believe, according to the working of His mighty power.

God wants us to learn to walk in His wisdom, knowledge, and power, that we may learn what are the riches of our inheritance in Christ Jesus. Before we can walk in the exceeding greatness of His power, we need the eyes of our understanding enlightened and we need Jesus's spirit of wisdom and revelation. This is why he left for us stories about Himself. If we listen to God's word and seek His face, He reveals to us little nuggets of truth; He shows us little pieces of Himself that help enlighten our eyes of understanding and gives us wisdom as we walk through our journey in life. First Corinthians 1:30 says that Jesus is made unto us wisdom, righteousness, sanctification, and redemption. Jesus is always flowing with divine wisdom and when we depend on Him, He makes wisdom to flow in us.

As we immerse ourselves in His word, God uses His stories and His faith pictures to minister unto us His wisdom and knowledge and to build us up in the faith. Romans 12:3 says that God has dealt each one of us a measure of faith. How do we grow that faith? We encourage ourselves in the word, we speak the word, and we receive every promise and every faith picture as our own. Jesus is the same yesterday, today, and forever. If He healed once, He will heal again. If He blessed once, He will bless again. If He provided a miracle once, He will provide a miracle again. If He prospered once, He will prosper again. Our part is to believe what He says and to believe He will do what He says.

We have not because we ask not. And sometimes we ask not because we don't know that we can ask. Or sometimes we ask so small because we don't know that it delights Him when we ask big. Many of us spend years not knowing what are the riches of our inheritance in Jesus as blood-bought heirs of the Most High God. If there is a blessing, an inheritance, a healing that is stored up for me in heaven, a storehouse with my name on it, I want to know about it, and I want to receive it.

For instance, I read in Psalm 23, "The Lord is my shepherd I shall not want" (v. 1). What God is saying is that He is our God of more than enough, and it is His desire that we shall not lack. When the Lord told Peter to let down his nets, Jesus filled the nets to bursting (Luke 5:4–7). After Jesus rose from the dead, a similar incident happened. Again, Jesus told the disciples to cast out their nets on the right side of the boat and the nets were so full they could not lift them in the boat, but had to drag them to shore (John 21:6–11). When He fed more than five thousand with two small fish and five loaves of bread, there were twelve baskets of leftovers (John 6:1–13). When God healed the lepers, they didn't wear the scars of it for the rest of their lives; He made their flesh fresher than a child's (Luke 17:12-14). When God restores, it is better than before (Job 33:25). When Jesus turned the water to wine, He didn't make a new wine or a mediocre wine; He made a fine wine, as if it had been aged for years (John. 2:3–10). Jesus never blesses by half-measures; he blesses in net-breaking, boat-sinking, beyond what you could think or ask measures. The Lord says to us, "Because I am your Shepherd, you shall not lack."

Some preachers try to convince us that we shouldn't really bother God with our heart's desires because it is enough that God provides just our basic needs. But that is not what my Bible says. Ephesians 3:20 says, "Now to Him who is able to do exceedingly abundantly above all that we ask or think, according to the power that works in us." First John 5:15 says, "And if we know that He hears us, whatever we ask, we know that we have the petitions that we have asked of Him." Psalm 37:4 says, "Delight yourself also in the LORD, and He shall give you the desires of your heart." God also says in Numbers 23:19 that God is not a liar and that which He says, He will do. This should fill us with hope and enthusiasm, that if God says it, then we can have every confidence that He will bring it to pass. That is why it behooves us to know what He says about us. Let's begin expanding our faith by exploring some of God's truths revealed through His faith pictures.

Revelation

Once I did not see how Bible stories were relevant, but now I know that every type, shadow, similitude, and faith picture reveals something about my Heavenly Father's love for me.

Prayer of Praise

Thank you, Lord, for Your Word, for Your promises, and for Your faith pictures. Lord, allow me to see and understand more about You, and more about Your great love for me. Lord, I want to grow in Your wisdom, knowledge, truth, and grace. I want to know more about You so I can become all that I am supposed to be. Make me a blessing, Lord, to my family and to all those around me. Help me to become a living testimony of Your faith pictures, bringing to life Your truths and making You real to my family and friends. O Lord, fill me with Your wisdom, knowledge, and power and make me Your blessed shekinah to my family and to the world.

Leah and Rachel, Martha and Mary: Grace Trumps Law

Grace trumps law. The law kills, but the Spirit gives life. When Moses brought the Ten Commandments down from Mt. Sinai, three thousand people perished (Exod. 32:28). When the Holy Spirit descended at Pentecost, three thousand souls got saved (Acts 2:41). Paul calls the law "the ministry of death" and "the ministry of condemnation" (2 Cor. 3:7–9). He says, "I was alive once without the law, but when the commandment came, sin revived and I died. And the commandment, which was to bring life, I found to bring death" (Rom. 7:9–10). The law demands from man what is impossible to give, whereas grace supplies to man what is impossible to earn. The law was a yoke, a wearisome burden, whereas grace is a gift, a wonderful blessing. What a blessed revelation it was for me to realize that I am no longer dead under the law but alive under grace!

So many young believers, like I was, get stuck in the law and end up completely blinded to grace. When we read the grace passages, we assume they are for someone else and not for those like us who don't measure up. We are wooed to the Lord with the language of grace, but then well-meaning pastors and teachers heap upon us the full language of the law, thrusting us into a centrifuge of self-effort and failure, which rapidly spirals into a pit of discouragement, condemnation, and despair.

The law demands righteousness from sinfully bankrupt man, whereas grace imparts to us Jesus's righteousness as a gift to man. The law reveals what man ought to be but can never achieve, whereas grace reveals who God is and what He has already accomplished. The law is man-centered and works-based, whereas grace is Jesus-centered and faith-based. The law tells us what we must do for God, whereas grace tells us what Jesus has already done for us. The law puts all the focus on man and his works, whereas grace puts all the focus on Jesus and what He has done for us through His finished work on the cross. The law demands, whereas grace supplies.

God made two different covenants with man, one based on the law of God, and the other based on the grace of God. Most of us are probably familiar with the story of Jacob and his two wives, Leah and Rachel. When Jacob had to run from his brother, Esau, who was angry because Jacob had cheated him out of his birth right, Jacob ran to the land of his relatives in Haran. As he was inquiring as to where his uncle Laban lived, he met Laban's daughter Rachel, who was bringing her father's sheep to a nearby well for water. Jacob saw Rachel and fell madly in love with her. He asked his uncle's permission to wed Rachel and agreed to work seven years for Laban in return for Rachel's hand in marriage.

On his wedding night, his uncle got him drunk and then switched brides on Jacob, giving him the older sister, Leah. The next morning, when he realized he had been tricked, it was too late. Consequently, Jacob had to work another seven years to win the hand of his true love; therefore, he ended up with two wives, one that he loved and adored and one he didn't.

The story of Leah and Rachel is a faith picture of the two covenants God cut with man. Leah, the older sister, represents the law, which was given at Mt. Sinai; and Rachel, the younger sister, represents grace, which came to Mt. Zion in Jerusalem. *Leah* in Hebrew means "weary" because one gets "weary" trying to keep the law. When one tries to earn one's own righteousness through self-effort, it is exhausting and wearisome. *Rachel* in Hebrew means "ewe" or "female sheep," which is a picture of the sacrificial Lamb of God that takes away the sin of the world. Her name is a picture of grace. A sacrificial lamb in the Old Testament stood in the place of the one who offered it. The lamb receives the penalty of laws demands and gives its life in order to redeem the one who brings the offering.

In Genesis, it is implied that Leah was not very attractive, just like the law is not attractive to those under its yoke of bondage. We also know that Jacob did not love Leah, the same way that God does not love the law. The law was given to show man how far he falls short of God's holy standards. But if God loved the law, He would not have made room for a second covenant. Rachel, on the other hand, was beautiful, just like His grace is beautiful to all those who experience it. We know that Jacob loved and adored Rachel, the same way God loves and adores us and gave His own Son to die for us. Jesus loved us so much that He willingly laid down His life to become our Lamb of God.

Leah can also mean to be disgusted, to grieve, to faint, and to loath. All who try through self-effort to keep the law end up disgusted with themselves and ultimately believe God is disgusted with them, because no matter how hard they try, they end up failing and falling short. All those who try to live up to the law end up grieving over their wretchedness and sinful behaviors that they cannot seem to overcome. Some of us nearly faint for want of trying so hard, yet, ultimately, we end up loathing ourselves for our inability to live a holy sinless life. When we focus on our flesh and our works, it makes us sin-conscious, and we end up doing the very thing we are so focused on trying not to do. The law makes us sin-conscious and flesh-focused. Like Paul said, "For the good that I will to do, I do not do; but the evil I will not to do, that I practice" (Rom. 7:19).

For those married to the law, it is like lowering a veil of darkness over one's eyes. When we center all our focus on self, on our works, on our efforts, and on our holiness, or lack thereof, the Bible says, we will not be able to understand the truth or see God's glory because only in Christ is the veil lifted and taken away. Paul says,

> But their minds were blinded. For until this day
> the same veil remains unlifted in the reading of

the Old Testament, because the veil is taken away in Christ. But even to this day, when Moses is read, a veil lies on their heart. Nevertheless when one turns to the Lord, the veil is taken away. Now the Lord is the Spirit; and where the spirit of the Lord is, there is liberty. But we all, with unveiled face, beholding as in a mirror the glory of the Lord, are being transformed into the same image from glory to glory, just as by the Spirit of the Lord. (2 Corinthians 3:14–18)

At the moment Christ died, the veil in the temple was torn in two because God was telling us that Christ has taken away the veil that stands between us and the Father. He is telling us that once the Holy Spirit takes up residence in our hearts, we have direct access to the Father as sons and daughters of the Most High. Through the Holy Spirit, we have liberty to come before the Father with unveiled faces because Jesus in us is the face the Father sees. As we worship and adore Jesus, beholding Him as in a mirror, we are being transformed into His image from glory to glory.

The knowledge of holiness and God does not come by the law, for by the law is the knowledge of sin; it comes by adoring and beholding Jesus, our righteousness. Romans 3:20–22 states:

Therefore by the deeds of the law no flesh will be justified in His sight, for by the law is the knowledge of sin. But now the righteousness of God apart from the law is revealed, being witnessed by the Law and the Prophets, even the righteousness of God, through faith in Jesus Christ, to all and on all who believe.

The glory of God was restored to man through the gift of the cross and can only be accessed through His Grace; whereas, those blinded by the veil of the law cannot see God's glory or enter into His Grace. Those under the Lord's ministry of mercy have renounced the hidden things of shame and walk in the redeeming light of the gospel of the glory of Christ, who is the image of God, and who shines His Shekinah Glory and Divine Radiance upon us. As we behold Christ and all His Glory, we are being transformed into His likeness. That is the power of His Grace and why it is so much more powerful and precious than the law ever was or could be.

Rachel can also mean to journey. Female ewes were the dominant element of a flock, and they were the best travelers. When Grace came in the Person of Jesus Christ, we can rest in the fact that we were assured a victorious journey through life. We may have setbacks, but setbacks are merely springboards for comebacks. We can have confidence because we are loved and adored and God tells us it is His heart to bless us. We can hold our heads high (Ps. 3:3) knowing that as Jesus is right now, exalted, full of glory, and lifted up, seated at the right hand of the Father, so are we (1 John 4:17).

When we belong to Jesus, we are his sheep, we belong to His flock, and because of Him, because we are the righteousness of God in Christ, we become the dominant one in our flock, in our families, in our workplace, in our journey through life. His favor chases after us and hunts us down (Ps. 23:6). We can expect preferential treatment. If Jesus is for me, who can stand against me (Rom. 8:31)? As a beloved and adored daughter of the Most High, I can expect goodness and blessings from my Heavenly Father's hand. He makes my paths smooth and my journey a joy.

Leah represents old wineskins, and Rachel new wineskins. We are cautioned not to put new wine into old wineskins because it will cause them to burst. The Lord is telling us to not mix the two covenants. God found fault with the old covenant otherwise He would not have made provision for a new one (Heb. 8:7–9). It was God who made the first covenant obsolete. "Now what is becoming obsolete and growing old is ready to vanish away" (Heb. 8:13). Man is the one who keeps trying to put new wine into the old wineskins.

Man is the one who wants to hang onto and resurrect the law. The law appeals to our vanity. It puts all the focus on us and our works. It relies on our ability to perform. This is comforting to those who feel that they must be in control, or to those who feel they have to do something to earn God's favor. The thing is, we cannot earn His favor through works, because it is a free gift, solely based on Jesus's obedience. Sad to say, law keepers often end up the most critical, harsh, judgmental people, because not only do they put law's demands on themselves, but they apply it even more harshly to others. To cling to the old covenant means Christ died in vain; it makes all the blessings of God that are ours because of the cross null and void.

Under the old covenant you are blessed and cursed. If you obey, you are blessed; but if you disobey you are cursed, even to the third and fourth generation. And if you fail in just one aspect of the law, you are guilty of breaking the whole law. James said, "For whosoever shall keep the whole law, and yet stumble in one point, he is guilty of all" (James 2:10). If you want to be under the old covenant, then you cannot pick and choose which laws you may keep. There is no grace under the law. You have to keep all of it if you want to be blessed, or, if you fail, then cursing is certain. There was no way for us to be blessed under the law, because ultimately, we all fail. I am so relieved that the yoke of the law is no longer ours to bear. "For the law of the Spirit of life in Christ Jesus has set you free from the law of sin and of death" (Rom. 8:1–2). Praise God!

Under the new covenant we are made righteous because of Jesus's obedience at the cross. He lived a perfect sinless life and then offered his own body as our sacrificial Lamb, so we could become spotless in His sight. Jesus's blood covers us completely, so that when our Heavenly Father looks at us, all He sees is Jesus's sinless perfection. God no longer sees us in the weaknesses of our flesh, He only sees us perfected and sanctified through His Precious Son.

He assures us, "For I will be merciful to their unrighteousness, and their sins and their lawless deeds I will remember no more"

(Heb. 8:12; Jer. 31:31–34). In Psalms, God says, "For as the heavens are high above the earth, so great is His mercy toward those who fear Him; as far as the east is from the west, so far has He removed our transgressions from us" (Ps. 103:11–12). Under His grace, we are entirely cleansed and sanctified.

Under the new covenant, we can only be blessed. Jesus took all our curses in his own body so that we will never be cursed again. "Christ has redeemed us from the curse of the law, having become a curse for us (for it is written, 'Cursed is everyone who hangs on a tree'" (Gal. 3:13). God made Him who knew no sin to become sin for us, that we might become the righteousness of God in Him (2 Cor. 5:21).

Proverbs tells us, "Blessings are on the head of the righteous" (Prov. 10:6), and Psalms declares, "The blessings of the Lord makes one rich" (Ps. 10:22). In Deuteronomy, He tells us, "Therefore know that the Lord your God, He is God, the faithful God who keeps covenant and mercy for a thousand generations with those who love Him and keep His commandments" (7:9). The Bible is filled with scriptures, teachings, and faith pictures on all the blessing that are ours in Christ Jesus, which will be revealed in the chapters to come.

The story of Mary and Martha is also a beautiful picture of law and grace. For many women, we either relate to one of the personality types or the other. In the modern love languages phraseology, Martha was an "acts of service" person and Mary was probably a "words" person. For those women who are Marthas, they fully empathize with Martha's plight. She was hosting the Lord and hustling about trying to get a meal prepared, while her sister, Mary, was sitting at Jesus's feet, listening to His every word. Martha got exasperated with her sister for not helping her and asked the Lord to chide her into getting back to work. Jesus answered Martha by saying, "Martha, Martha, you are worried and troubled about many things. But one thing is needed, and Mary has chosen the better part, which will not be taken away from her" (Luke 10:41–42).

For an "acts of service" person, this advice does not seem at all practical. Matter of fact, I used to find myself annoyed by this response. Who is going to get the dinner on if we are all sitting at Jesus's feet soaking up His every word? After all, Martha invited the Lord to her house; therefore, she is expected by tradition and decent manners to produce a meal. So let's be real here—someone has to cook! Or do they? Martha would have known that the Lord had healed many, chased out demons, raised the dead, and had fed over five thousand with five loaves and two small fish, yet still had twelve baskets of leftovers. Did the Lord really need Martha's service? She thought so at the time, but if she would have sat down with her sister, the Lord would have provided the rest.

Martha is a quiet reminder from the Lord that He doesn't need our service. We should serve because it results out of an overflowing of joy and gratitude for all that Jesus has done for us, not as an act of duty. If we feel obligated to serve, then we are putting ourselves under the law by trying to earn God's favor. Again, we cannot earn His favor. It is a gift. We have favor solely based on what Christ accomplished on our behalf. It has nothing to do with our works and our performance. If we can earn grace, then it is not a gift. If grace is a gift, then it is not wages. Romans says, "For the wages of sin is death, but the gift of God is eternal life in Christ Jesus our Lord" (Rom. 6:23). Under the law, it is our duty to serve; but under grace, it is our privilege to serve, yet our main responsibility is to receive.

Was Jesus most flattered by Martha's duty to serve or Mary's willingness to receive? Under the new covenant, how do we work the works of God? In John, "Jesus answered and said to them, 'This is the work of God that you believe in Him whom He sent'" (6:28–29). Our part under the new covenant is to believe in God's Son. For many of us, this means we invite Jesus into our heart, and then we serve in our local church, which is a Martha outlook. For others, this means not only do I invite Jesus into my heart but I also believe everything He says about me, and I hang my faith on His every Word. This means I receive every word, every promise, every blessing, and every faith picture as mine, which is a Mary outlook. Martha serves; whereas Mary receives. The law demands, whereas grace supplies.

The law keeps the law keeper from grace. "You have been estranged from Christ. You who attempt to be justified by the law; you have fallen from Grace" (Gal. 5:4). Grace, on the other hand, gives the believer access to every blessing of God. "Therefore, having been justified by faith, we have peace with God through our Lord Jesus Christ, through whom also we have access by faith into this grace in which we stand, and rejoice in hope of the glory of God" (Rom. 5:1–2). Grace exalts us from "slaves to sin" to "heirs of God." "For the promise that he would be heir of the world was not to Abraham or to his seed through the law, but through the righteousness of faith" (Rom. 4:13). We enter into His grace through faith, not by the works of the law.

Did God credit Abraham with marvelous works? Is he remembered for his perfect sinless behavior? In Romans, we read, "What then shall we say that Abraham our father has found according to the flesh? For if Abraham was justified by works, he has something to boast about, but not before God. For what does the Scripture say? 'Abraham believed God, and it was accounted to him for righteousness'" (Rom. 4:1–3). Abraham lived long before the law was given. He found favor in the eyes of the Lord because Abraham believed God. That is all he did; he believed God.

As with Abraham, God made a covenant with us based on His grace, and all he wants from us is to believe Him, to believe in the Son whom He sent, to believe what He says about us, and to believe that He will do what He says. He wants us to be firmly rooted in the belief that His grace, His perfect sacrifice and divine favor, has fulfilled the law (Rom. 13:10).

His grace breaks the power of sin over the believer's life and liberates us to live victoriously. The Bible states that sin shall not have dominion over those who are under grace (Rom. 6:14). God also tells us that as we grow in His grace and the knowledge of Jesus Christ that we are progressively transformed into His image from glory to glory (2 Cor. 3:18). As we look at Jesus, it is like looking in a mirror so that the more we look to, adore, and worship Him, the more we are transformed into His image. Under His holy blood, we are made 100 percent righteous, but under His glorious grace, we grow in holiness as He gives us His wisdom and power to live victorious lives.

Under the new covenant, it is 100 percent about what Jesus has accomplished for us at the Cross. It is 100 percent Jesus's finished work that qualifies us for every blessing of God. It is 100 percent due to Jesus's righteousness that we can come boldly unto the throne of Grace. It is 100 percent Jesus that God sees when He looks at us. God can love us 100 percent with all His heart without a single reservation because we are found 100 percent accepted in His sight thanks to His precious gift of Grace. We are 100 percent loved, 100 percent adored, 100 percent favored, 100 percent blessed, and 100 percent forgiven. For those of us who believe God, we are 100 percent thankful that His glorious grace trumps the law.

Revelation
Once I was blind, but now I see.

Prayer of Praise
Lord, thank You for opening my eyes to Your Grace and removing the veil of the law. Lord, make me more of a Mary and not a Martha. Lord, I want to sit at Your feet and hear Your voice, to not get swallowed up in the busyness of everyday life. Lord, I want to be an emissary of Your Grace, not a harbinger of the law with its criticism and judgment. Lord, make me strong when I need to be firm and make me gracious, gentle, and understanding when compassion and empathy are required. Help me, O Lord, to measure my words carefully, offering encouragement and grace, not condemnation and negativity. When I must correct, make me loving in my criticism. Teach me the art of using tactful words—words that foster health, life, joy, and peace. Make me like You, Lord, full of mercy and grace.

Ruth: Redeemed and Restored

July 28, 2010, my mother—my precious friend, my rock of security, safety, and steadfast source of love and affirmation—passed away. Now I have no rock to fall back on, to depend on in emergencies, no safety net whatsoever. I felt so alone, so abandoned, so orphaned. Now, not only am I an older woman who is chronically underemployed and stuck in the worst recession since the Great Depression, but I am also motherless. I feel so lost, so forsaken, so forgotten. Everything in me wants to curl up into a ball, go to sleep, and never wake up. My heart feels as though it will explode under the strain of troubles, trials, and sorrows. I am so discouraged, so sad, and so depressed that I cannot drum up any desire, any reason, let alone the energy, to go on. The only person who had faith in me is gone. My greatest champion is gone. How will I carry on?

Then it dawned on me—in the same way that my mother was my rock, my children will look to me to be their rock. I need to carry on so I can be their rock of support and strength in times of need. I can't fall apart or give up, because they are looking to me to be the steady one, the strong one. I must be for them everything my mother was to me. This thought sparks hope. I still have a purpose on this planet, a reason to wake up. God is not done with me yet. So I got up. I put one foot in front of the other, and I was determined to carry on, to get through this sorrow, and to doggedly move forward and survive this soul-crushing grief. To be sure, those were the darkest days of my life, but then Grace came.

Grace came and revealed to my heart that I still have a champion, that Jesus believes in me, that He is my Rock, and that He is irrevocably for me. It might look bad, it may feel bad, and it may be bad, but since I belong to Jesus, I have His word that it will not stay bad. He promises that He takes everything man or Satan means for evil against me and He actively turns it to my good. My part is to hear Him and to believe what He says (Matt. 17:5). When the Lord Jesus was transfigured, a voice came out of the cloud saying, "This is My beloved Son. Hear Him!" (Luke 9:35) Thanks to His glorious grace, I finally heard Him.

I heard, "You are My beloved!" I heard, "You are My heavenly princess, My royal priestess!" I heard, "You are My beloved daughter, My precious shekinah! With Me all things are possible!" I heard, "You sit with Me at My Father's right hand, beneath the mighty wings of the Cherubim, and all power and authority in heaven and earth has been given unto you in Jesus's name. As Jesus is right now, exalted and lifted up, so are you!" Forty years after being saved, I finally heard Jesus's words of grace and I believed Him. This time my tears were ones of joy, because, finally, I heard and I believed that I am fully redeemed and completely restored, that my Jesus is my champion and He puts the whole universe on my side. Since He is for me, what do I possibly have to fear?

Jesus is our Kinsman-Redeemer, and He promises to restore unto us all the years the locusts have eaten. It doesn't matter how bleak or how hopeless our circumstances may look, we have God's assurance that He has redeemed us unto Himself (2 Sam. 7:23). He has redeemed our souls from destruction (Ps. 34:22; 49:15; 69:18; 103:4). He promises to restore to us all those wasted years, those wasted opportunities, and those wasted relationships, and He supernaturally turns it all to our favor. He restores our soul, our identity of all that we are in Him (Ps. 23:3); He restores our joy (Ps. 51:12); He restores our comforts (Is. 57:18); He restores double, quadruple, and quintuple for all that we have lost (Exod. 22:4; Luke 19:8; 2 Sam. 12:6); He restores our health (Jer. 30:17); our years (Joel 2:25); our youth

(Ps. 103:5); our beauty (1 Pet. 3:6); our wholeness (Matt. 12:13); our lives from the dead (2 Kings 8:1; John 11:43-44; Rom. 4:17). We also know that when God restores, it is better than before, either in quality or quantity. So it may look bad, feel bad, and be bad, but the final chapter has not been written. Jesus, our Kinsman-Redeemer, has the final word, not our circumstances.

When we belong to the Lord, we have His assurance that it will not stay bad. Our job is to take our eyes off our circumstances and put them onto Jesus and to believe what He says about us. God said, "I will never leave you nor forsake you" (Heb. 13:5). God said, "For You, O LORD, will bless the righteous; with favor; You will surround him as with a shield" (Ps. 5:12). God said He will be a restorer of life and a nourisher of our old age (Ruth 4:15). Jesus redeems our souls, our years, our possessions, our health, our fears, our relationships, and He rescues us to the uttermost. We may not see His redemption of our negative circumstance today, tomorrow, or even a month from now, but if we keep our eyes on Jesus, He will turn things around for us.

The story of Ruth is a beautiful faith picture of how God delights in turning around our negative and seemingly hopeless circumstances. In Bible times, nothing could be worse than to lose all one's male relatives, because they were the providers. They did not have food stamps or social programs to cover people if they found themselves temporarily out of work; neither was there any kind of provision for widows and orphans. If you did not have family to take you in, your situation could indeed be desperate.

During a severe famine in the land of Judah, Elimelech, his wife Naomi, and their two sons moved to the country of Moab. Their sons grew up in Moab and eventually married Moabite women, Orpah and Ruth. Shortly after his sons married, Elimelech died. About ten years later, both of Naomi's sons died. As widows Naomi, Orpah, and Ruth were suddenly struck destitute and penniless. Orpah went home to her family, but Ruth would not desert her mother-in-law. Even though Naomi entreated her to return to her people, she would not leave Naomi comfortless and without support. Ruth spoke the words we so often hear at weddings:

> Entreat me not to leave you or to turn back from following you; for wherever you go, I will go; and wherever you lodge, I will lodge; your people shall be my people, and your God, my God. Where you die, I will die, and there will I be buried. The LORD do so to me, and more also, if anything but death parts you and me. (Ruth 1:16–17)

Naomi had no choice but to return to her hometown of Bethlehem so she could seek the shelter and assistance of her family. Ruth faithfully escorted Naomi back to her homeland.

They arrived in Bethlehem at the time of the barley harvest and Ruth asked Naomi if she could go to the fields to glean grain. In those days, poor people could walk behind the reapers and pick up any grain that happened to fall to the ground. She happened to come to one of the fields that belonged to Boaz, a wealthy relative of Naomi's. Boaz saw Ruth, inquired from his men as to whom she was, and then he spoke to her and instructed Ruth to stay in his fields and to remain close to his young women. He instructed his men not to molest her, to let extra grain fall for her to reap, and to allow her to drink from the workers' water vessels.

Upon receiving such gracious consideration from Boaz, Ruth fell to her face and bowed down to the ground in front of him and asked why she, a foreigner, had found favor with him. He said that he had heard how much Ruth had done for her mother-in-law, how she had left her own father and mother to come with Naomi to a people she did not know. Then Boaz blessed Ruth and invited her to eat lunch with him. Ruth gleaned until it got dark. After she beat out the grain, she returned to the city and handed Naomi about four gallons of barley and also offered her some leftover lunch that she had saved for her.

Naomi asked where she had gleaned, and Ruth told her about Boaz's generosity toward her. Naomi responded, "Blessed be the LORD, who has not forsaken His kindness to the living and the dead!" (Ruth 2:20) She explained to Ruth that Boaz was a very near relative and that perhaps there was hope that he might redeem them. To redeem in Bible times meant that it fell to the nearest male relative to marry young widows and to raise an heir in the dead husband's name. Naomi told her that it was good news that Boaz had instructed Ruth to stay close to his young women and to glean only in his fields, so Ruth continued to glean in Boaz's fields until the end of the barley harvest.

Then one evening, Naomi told Ruth to get dolled up. Naomi instructed Ruth to go where Boaz was working at the threshing floor, wait until after he had eaten and had lain down, then she was to uncover his feet and to lie down and then wait until Boaz told her what to do. Ruth replied to Naomi, "All that you say to me I will do" (Ruth 3:5). Around midnight, Boaz woke up startled to find that there was someone lying at his feet. He quietly asked, "Who are you?" Ruth softly answered, "I am Ruth, your maidservant. Please take your maidservant under your wing, for you are a close relative." Then he said, "Blessed are you of the LORD, my daughter! For you have shown more kindness at the end than at the beginning, in that you did not go after young men, whether poor or rich" (Ruth 3:9–10). Boaz assured Ruth that he would do what she requested, although there was a closer relative who had the first right to redeem Ruth, so Boaz would have to give him first option, yet if he declined, then Boaz promised to redeem her. He instructed her to sleep until morning, and then at first light, he loaded her shawl with barley and sent her back to the city.

First thing that same morning, Boaz went to the city, gathered ten elders, and then found his relative sitting at the city gates. Boaz asked him if he would be willing to buy all the land that belongs to Naomi and her sons, which also meant he would have to redeem the widow Ruth, the Moabitess. The relative declined, so Boaz proclaimed in front of the ten witnesses that he would buy all the land that belonged to Naomi and that he would redeem Ruth and take her as his wife. The witnesses and all the people nearby who had heard Boaz's declaration rejoiced with him, and wished him many blessings. Boaz returned to Naomi's house and asked Ruth to marry him.

The LORD gave Ruth conception right away and she bore a son, and the women said to Naomi,

> "Blessed be the LORD, who has not left you this day without a close relative; and may his name be famous in Israel! And may he be to you a restorer of life and a nourisher of your old age; for your daughter-in-law loves you, who is better to you than seven sons, has borne him." Then Naomi took the child and laid him on her bosom, and became a nurse to him. Also the neighbor women called his name Obed. He is the father of Jesse, the father of David. (Ruth 4:14–17)

Boaz is the son of Rahab the harlot and Salmon of the tribe of Judah. Rahab was the Gentile woman who helped the two spies who were scoping out the city of Jericho for Joshua. Boaz was a person of mixed race and probably suffered his share of prejudice because of it. He undoubtedly had a soft spot for Ruth because she was a Gentile from another country, as was his mother. He also recognized and admired Ruth's loyalty and devotion to her mother-in-law. He was so impressed that Ruth was willing to leave her own mother and father and her own country to follow Naomi to a foreign land. This speaks to what kind of woman Naomi must have been to have earned such adoration and devotion from her daughter-in-law. Ruth's character is like so many godly women that we know. She is faithful, devoted, loyal, and self-sacrificing toward those whom she loves.

Ruth loved Naomi so much she did not have the heart to desert her in her hour of need. When Naomi lost her husband and her two sons, she lost all the security she had in the world. As an older woman, she undoubtedly had some limitations as to what she could do to earn her own bread, which may no longer have even been possible for her. Ruth would know that without the strength of a younger woman who still had the ability to work a menial job like cooking, sewing, or gleaning in the fields, Naomi would likely starve to death. It doesn't sound like any close relatives took her in, so she would have been dependent on Ruth. Typically, when young women were widowed, they went back to their family to live, and their family would try to find another husband for them.

Ruth would have known that as a foreigner, she may not be very well received in Naomi's country, but she was committed to go with her regardless. A woman of no faith may have resigned herself to the fact that she may have to spend the rest of her days as a childless widow, but I believe Ruth had heard enough about Naomi's God to know that He was a God of miracles, and that with Him all things were possible. We do know that she followed Naomi's instructions, as odd as they were. That tells us that she trusted Naomi, and more importantly, she trusted Naomi's God. It is obvious from Scripture that God was directing Ruth's steps. She happened to come to the field of Boaz. He happened to notice her, and he happened to hear wonderful things about her. These happenings are not accidents but the handiwork of a loving God.

Our Heavenly Father puts us in the right place at the right time. He orders our steps and makes our way successful. There is no such thing as luck; with God it is called favor. He orchestrates times and events to work in our favor. "The steps of a good man are ordered by the LORD; and He delights in his way. Though he fall, he shall not be utterly cast down; For the LORD upholds him with His hand" (Ps. 37:23–24). I believe Naomi would have told Ruth all the wonderful stories about the mighty God of Israel, who parted the Red Sea, who fed her people with manna from the sky, who made mighty fortresses like Jericho crumble with just a shout, and who provided for His people in miraculous ways. I believe Ruth was a lot like us.

She found herself in an extremely negative situation, but she knew that her God was bigger than all of that, and that He would come through for them.

You know it takes more energy to indulge fear and worry than it does to believe God. I have never been more miserable, exhausted, and at the end of my self than when I have fretted and freaked out over negative circumstances, as compared to believing what God says and placing my faith and confidence in His goodness toward me. Before I understood His grace, I believed God's intentions toward me were sinister, that He was seeking ways to torment me. Of course, I panicked over trials and tribulations because I was convinced that God was out to get me, that He was going to make me suffer and pay for every sin, and who can stand against an angry Almighty God? Oh how dark our minds can sink when we are under the lies of the accuser of the brethren! No pit is too low, no darkness so black, as when Satan has us entwined in his ugly snares of deception!

Jesus says, "My yoke is easy and my burden is light" (Matt. 11:30). How true! When we know the truth that God is actually for us, that He has legions of angels working on our behalf 24/7—that God is moving heaven and earth for us—our burden becomes light! Our heart is full to bursting with joy because we have the confidence that He is working everything out for our good. So even when the circumstance is still there, it is not a death sentence; it is merely a temporary challenge or setback that is about to change. That is faith! That is hope! Faith is the substance of things hoped for, the evidence of things not seen! I may not see it yet, but faith believes and declares, my blessing is on the way—my healing is on the way—my provision is on the way! Thank you, Jesus!

Do you see that when we have God's perspective on our circumstance, when we are operating out of faith, how optimistic we feel about our trials and challenges as opposed to having Satan's perspective, which is all doom, gloom, fear, depression, and discouragement? It takes more energy to place our faith in Satan's lies than it does to place our faith in God's word. One stirs us up to worry, fretfulness, anxiety, fear, turmoil, and misery; whereas the other imparts hope, optimism, encouragement, confidence, and joy. Satan loves to jerk us around like a rag doll, provoking us to fear and every negative imagining; whereas Jesus promises us that greater is He that is in us than he that is in the world (1 John 4:4). We have God's promise that no weapon formed against us shall prosper (Isa. 54:17). The Bible doesn't say there won't be weapons waged or angry attacks or challenging circumstances, but He promises us and gives us His assurance that they will not prosper against us. They will not win because greater is He that is in us than he who is trying to bedevil us. God has all His hosts of heaven working on our behalf. This should fill us with confidence, hope, and joy!

Ruth would have grown up in a fear-based, works-based religion where all one's focus is on pleasing the gods and not angering the gods. What a relief for Ruth to learn that there is only one true God and that it is His heart to bless and provide for His people! The Jews were God's chosen people, and He fought for them and brought them into a land of milk and honey. He gave them lands for which they did not labor; houses, fences, and barns that they did not build; and pastures, vineyards, and gardens that they did not plant (Josh. 24:13). He blessed those who blessed His people and cursed those who cursed His people. He was loving and invincible, and Naomi's God was now Ruth's God. She would have had every confidence that her God would supply her need. Even more amazing is that when God supplies, it is more than we could possibly think or ask.

Boaz is a picture of Jesus, our Kinsman-Redeemer, who is not only willing, but He has the power to redeem and restore us. Like Ruth, when we fall at the feet of Jesus, we place ourselves in a position for healing and restoration. At the feet of Jesus, all things are possible. Everyone who came to Him received His healing, blessings, and restoration. No one was turned away. No one left empty-handed. All who fell at His feet received what they came for. Not only is it His heart to bless us, it is His greatest pleasure to prosper us. When we delight in Jesus, God delights in giving us the desires of our hearts; He takes great joy in granting us the secret petitions of our hearts.

Ruth ended up with one of the wealthiest bachelors in Bethlehem. Her proposal of marriage exalted her from pauper status to princess status. Naomi was exalted from old-washed-up-forgotten-widow status to grandmother-and-nursemaid-to-a-prince status. Not only did they have the supreme blessing of being given a son and grandson, Obed is named in the line of Christ. He wasn't just any baby; he was predestined to be the grandfather of David, the future king of Israel. What an honor! What a blessing! So beyond what anyone would think or ask! This is our God. He delights in restoring double, five-fold, twenty-five fold beyond what we could think or imagine. It is His heart to bless us and His greatest pleasure to prosper us. When we delight in His Son, He delights in lavishing on us the desires of our hearts. Set your eyes upon Jesus, hear Him, and watch Him redeem and restore your life to the uttermost.

Revelation

Once I felt my heart would explode under the strain of troubles and trials, but now I feel as though my heart will burst with joy and gratitude.

Prayer of Praise

Thank you, Lord, for redeeming my life from destruction, disease, and death. Apart from You, Lord, I am nothing, yet in You I am exalted far above every principality and power, and I am seated in heavenly places at Your right hand. You promised that You would be my God and that I would belong to You (Heb. 8:10). That means every miracle You ever worked belongs to me and nothing and no one can pluck me out of Your hand. I can expect miracles and blessings because You are my miracle-working God, the One who redeems, renews, restores, and manifests to me the fullness of Your glory and grace.

The Woman Caught in Adultery: The Gift of No Condemnation

Is there anyone who doesn't have things in their past that they are ashamed of? Who in the exuberance and foolishness of youth doesn't have a long and winding trail of mistakes? Of those who got saved quite young, who doesn't have a list a mile long of things they wished they had done differently? Is there anyone alive who does not have regrets? Although most people try their very best to be decent, law-abiding, moral human beings, this thing called "the flesh" ultimately gets in the way. Our very best intentions can fall flat, our noblest goals can get twisted and derailed, and our very best effort is sometimes just not good enough.

We live in a fallen world. We suffer attacks, wrongful accusations, and sometimes we just blow it, and there is no one to blame but ourselves. Sometimes we just plain old choose to sin. We fail and fall short because we are human. If we have breath, we have an unnerving unction to sin. How we choose to deal with our sin puts Christians in one of two camps; one group lives under fear, guilt, shame, condemnation, and judgment, whereas the other group has received the gift of no condemnation and judgment. Although both groups are saved, their response to their sin is completely different.

The people in the first group can often feel defeated, struggle with addictions, and can be paralyzed by fear of failure. When they look in the mirror, all they see is someone who does not measure up. Although they try with all their might to not sin, what they end up doing is the very thing they hate. Their experience is often an endless cycle of try and fail, try harder and fail, try their hardest and fail, and at the end of it all, the enemy of their soul heaps all manner of accusation upon them, convincing them that they are no better than pond scum in the eyes of God.

The people in the first group believe that sin has a consequence, and they beat themselves up terribly, some even to the extreme of self-injury, because they feel that is what they deserve. Mental institutions are filled with people who have literally made themselves mad over their shame, guilt, and self-condemnation. Among this group, self-hatred is pervasive, and it manifests itself in all manner of autoimmune diseases. Their self-hatred turns inward and begins to turn their own body against itself. This ugly realm of self-hatred, self-injury, self-disgust, and self-preoccupation is exactly where Satan delights in keeping us. He is that voice that is accusing us, mocking us, and belittling us, and the oxymoron here is that he uses the Scriptures to accuse us—he uses the law. Matter of fact, Satan loves the law, and he is an expert at wielding it against the brethren.

He'll say things like, "How dare you call yourself a Christian! Look what you just did! You…" and he lists the commandments that you broke. He will shame us by saying things like, "Boy, you are going to be so humiliated when you get to heaven, because God is going to play back your life on a giant movie screen for all of heaven to see, and everyone will see and know what a wretched, lowlife, scum-sucking worthless piece of **** you really are! That is what your God thinks of you! Better throw in the towel now, lady, because you are hopeless!" This group lives in utter deception, misery, hopelessness, and despair. I know because I used to be counted among their number.

The other group, the ones who have received the gift of no condemnation, deals with their sins and shortcomings in a completely different way. This group has received the gospel of grace into their hearts. These Christians know and believe that Jesus cut a new covenant with our Heavenly Father on our behalf and that He offered His own sinless blood as payment for our sin. They know and believe,

> Therefore, as through one man's offense (Adam) judgment came to all men resulting in condemnation, even so through one Man's righteous act the free gift came to all men, resulting in justification of life. For as by one man's disobedience many were made sinners, so also by one Man's obedience many will be made righteous. Moreover the law entered that the offense might abound. But where sin abounded, grace abounded much more, so that as sin reigned in death, even so grace might reign through righteousness to eternal life through Jesus Christ our Lord. (Romans 5:19–21)

These Christians receive that "God did not send His Son into the world to condemn the world, but that the world through Him might be saved. He who believes in Him is not condemned" (John. 3:17–18). This group believes that Jesus suffered immeasurable horrors to purchase our pardon, and our part under His new covenant is to receive this precious gift He has given us—the gift of salvation from sin's penalty and death, the gift of eternal life, and the gift of no condemnation.

The story of the woman caught in adultery is a precious faith picture of the Lord's heart toward His beloved. The Pharisees dragged out a woman who had been caught in the act of adultery and threw her at the feet of Jesus saying, "Now Moses, in the law, commanded us that such should be stoned. But what do you say?" (John. 8:5) They had hoped to trap Jesus into contradicting the law so they could arrest Him.

> Jesus stooped down and wrote on the ground with His finger, as though He did not hear. So when they continued asking Him, He raised Himself up and said to them, "He who is with-

out sin among you, let him throw the first stone." And again, He stooped down and wrote on the ground. (John 8:6–8)

Was He writing on the ground the various commandments he knew these men were guilty of breaking? The Bible doesn't say, but one by one, the crowd left, starting with the oldest and ending with the youngest. When Jesus and the woman were finally alone, He asked her, "Woman, where are those accusers of yours? Has no one condemned you?" She said, "No one, Lord." And Jesus said to her, "*Neither do I condemn you*; go and sin no more" (John 8:10–11, emphasis mine). Jesus told the woman, caught in the very act of sin, "Neither do I condemn you." Those words should penetrate our heart. Jesus is telling us, there is no condemnation for anyone who calls upon the name of Jesus.

When we look at Jesus's interaction with the Samaritan woman by Jacob's well, again, He did not express any condemnation toward the woman, only love. Unlike the Jews of His day, Jesus was not a respecter of persons, nor racially biased, for the woman was surprised that Jesus, a Jew, would even speak to her. Jews hated the Samaritans because they were a people of mixed race; they were only part Jewish. Jesus not only engaged her in conversation, but He led her to the saving knowledge of His grace. He knew that she had had five husbands, and that the man she was with now was not her husband, yet she received the Lord's gift of no condemnation. She went back into her city of Sychar and told the people all about the Christ, who had told her everything she had ever done, but still loved her. Jesus's gift of salvation includes the gift of no condemnation.

If anyone had the right to beat up and condemn himself, it would be Paul. While he was a zealous Pharisee, he had Christians beaten, imprisoned, and killed. Yet after he got saved, he would not let the errors of his past rob him of his joy in the Lord today. John wrote, "If anyone sins, we have an Advocate with the Father, Jesus

Christ the righteous. And He Himself is the propitiation (mercy seat) for our sins" (1 John 2:1–2). Paul said, "Brethren, I do not count myself to have apprehended; but one thing I do, forgetting those things which are behind and reaching forward to those things which are ahead, I press toward the goal for the prize of the upward call of God in Christ Jesus" (Phil. 3:13–14). We can't undo the past, but we can believe right today.

One insight God gave Joseph Prince is that right living is the result of right believing and our righteousness is not right doing, but right being. Romans 4:5 says, "But to him who does not work but believes on Him who justifies the ungodly, his faith is accounted for righteousness." If you believe you are under the law, then you become sin-focused and self-focused, giving sin a foothold in your life. If you believe that you are under Grace, then you are Jesus-focused and righteousness-focused, giving His righteousness a foothold in your life. "For as he thinks in his heart, so is he" (Prov. 23:7). The Bible tells us that God imputes righteousness to those who believe in His Son, not to those who strive to keep the law (Gal. 2:16). The moment we invite Jesus into our hearts, He takes our sins and gives us His righteousness (2 Cor. 5:21), and God sees us as righteous apart from our works, our obedience, or disobedience. Our righteousness comes by our faith, not by our works.

It requires faith to declare "I am the righteousness of God in Christ" right after we seriously blow it. It does not take faith to know when we have been ugly, foul, short-tempered, or rude. We all know when we have grieved the Holy Spirit or saddened our Savior by falling short of our high calling, yet it takes faith to proclaim our righteousness of God in Christ after our lowest moments. When Satan is screaming in our ear, "Look at what you just did! Look how you behaved! How dare you call yourself a Christian! You are such a disappointment to God!" It takes great faith in those moments to say "Lord, I am so sorry for my sin, and I thank you that I am the righteousness of my God in Christ." Like the woman caught in adultery, we could be caught in an all-time mortifying worst moment, one we deeply regret, but still, faith declares what Jesus has said about us and does not give heed to the enemy's harangue.

Jesus first told the woman caught in adultery, "Neither do I condemn thee," then He said, "Go and sin no more!" Before we can go and sin no more, we have to know that we are forgiven and loved. Once we are sure that God loves us, then we have the power to go and sin no more. The power of the cross breaks the power of sin over our lives. If we don't believe we are loved, on the contrary, we feel condemned and judged, then what good would it do to go and sin no more, for we would still be condemned and judged? That is why the old covenant is called the ministry of death, because there is no way to win. Once we have God's assurance of love and forgiveness, sin loses its foothold over our lives.

How we perceive God affects how we live and behave. If we see God as a great big ogre in the sky who is just waiting to smack us flat the minute we step out of line, then it makes us hyperfocused on our actions and our behavior. If we see God as our loving Heavenly Father who gave His one and only Son to die for us, to redeem us unto a right relationship with Himself, then it makes us hyperfocused on Jesus, on what He did for us. Jesus said, "Their sins and lawless deeds I will remember no more!" (Heb. 10:17) He says to us, "Neither do I condemn you!" (John 8:11). Right believing means I believe what God says about me. It means I believe every word, every promise, and every faith picture, then He gives me the power to go and sin no more. Believing right results in living right.

When we have really blown it and our conscience screams, "You are guilty! You deserve to be punished," we must be ready with God's answer to combat the voice of the enemy and to satisfy our guilty conscience. Be ready to declare "I am the righteousness of my God in Christ" (2 Cor. 5:21). Be armed with Hebrews 9:14, "How much more shall the blood of Christ, who through the eternal Spirit offered Himself without spot to God, cleanse your conscience from dead works to serve the living God?" God is telling us that Jesus offered Himself without spot, which means without a single blemish, flaw, misdeed, or sin, in order to cleanse our conscience from our dead and failing works. Our worth comes from our living Savior, not from our dead works. We are made acceptable to our Heavenly Father solely based on Jesus's righteousness, entirely apart from our works. Jesus suffered immeasurable horrors to cleanse our guilty conscience. If we hang onto and rehearse our past failures, then Jesus suffered in vain.

Jesus was brutally beaten and punished on account of our sins, and He suffered the fiery indignation of God's wrath in His own body for each of our transgressions, so that our guilty conscience is washed clean in the blood of the Lamb. When we refuse to forgive ourselves, then what was the point of His suffering? When we refuse to accept His gift of no condemnation, then we are just like the ones who spat on Him as He was carrying the cross of our shame up the hill of Golgotha. When we will not forgive ourselves, it is the same as saying, "Sorry, Jesus, but Your sacrifice just isn't enough for me! My sins are just too great for You. I know You said that God did not send You into the world to condemn the world, but that the world through You might be saved—but surely, I am the one special exception, right?"

Jesus emphatically declares, "No! That is not right! There are no exceptions! I cut a new covenant with God the Father that covers 'everyone' who believes. No matter how grievous the sin, it has been covered and paid for in full with My Holy blood. Therefore, there are absolutely no exceptions! I died once for all!"

So next time your conscience screams at you, ignore that voice and look to Jesus and say, "Thank you, Lord, that You suffered mightily on my behalf to cleanse me from the wretchedness of my sins. I am so sorry I blew it, Lord. I hate it when I let you down like that. I not only disappointed You, but I disappointed myself. I am so sorry, and I ask You to forgive me. Thank You, Jesus, that you bore all the lashings for my failures, therefore, my sin debt is paid. You were condemned on my behalf for this sin, so there is now absolutely no condemnation left for me. Thank You, that I have been set free from a guilty conscience thanks to Your finished work at the cross."

Jesus gives to each of us His gift of no condemnation. When God looks at us, He only sees His beloved Son. "Jesus loves me. This I know for the Bible tells me so." Oh, the grief we would be spared if we only believed the words to this childhood hymn. It sounds too simple. It is too simple, yet why did it take me forty years to believe this elementary Bible truth if it is so simple? Because we have an enemy to our souls, and like a roaring lion, he roams about seeking those whom he can devour. Whom does He devour? Those who do not believe that Jesus loves them—those who live under the curse of self-condemnation and judgment—all those who believe wrongly will be devoured, which results in fallen, fractured, fragile Christians, like I used to be. What a glorious revelation, indeed, for me to finally realize that there is no condemnation for those who are in Christ Jesus. That is the good news of the gospel. I am completely forgiven, past, present, and future, and in Christ Jesus, I will never again be condemned. The good news is, neither will you.

Revelation

Once I walked in shame, guilt, and condemnation, but now I walk in His unearned, undeserved, unbridled favor and blessing.

Prayer of Praise

Thank you, Jesus, that You paid the penalty, once and for all, for my sins on the cross two thousand years ago so that I could be forgiven and redeemed. You suffered grievously on my behalf so that I don't have to suffer for what I deserve. Thank You, Lord, for taking my beating and my death, so that You could give me Your complete forgiveness, Your eternal life, Your absolute victory, and Your perfect blessing. Thank You that Your great love and divine exchange raised a hopeless sinner like me to a beloved daughter of the Most High. Thank You for Your divine grace and favor that elevates me to the most exalted position in the universe, a blood-bought heir of God, which entitles me to every blessing and miracle of God.

Tamar: Victor, Not a Victim

For over forty years, I lived with a victim mentality. Satan had me convinced that God was against me; therefore, I lived under the belief that God didn't care about me, and that He was out to get me. I lived under the delusion that His justice and discipline meant that He would torment me with trials and tribulations. This mind-set threw me into survival mode. My part in dealing with sin's consequence was to persevere and survive the onslaught of negative circumstances until the day He takes me home. Life in this world was just something I had to endure. There was no joy, no hope, no way to win, for who can stand up against the righteous expectations of a holy God?

Since I inevitably failed, I felt I was a victim of His constant wrath and indignation, and my job was to learn my lessons quickly so I would survive the test. What a mind warp when I received the revelation that, although I deserve to be disciplined and punished for my sins, thanks to Jesus's finished work on the cross, I don't get what I deserve—I get what Jesus deserves! Once I was so very blind, but now I see; I am a victor, more than a conqueror in Christ, not a victim.

The Bible is filled with stories of strong women; women who had the wisdom to believe God and trust in His great love for them. Once we embrace the truth of how very much God loves us, it is so incredibly empowering. Great things happen. Powerful changes occur. Blessings gloriously abound. He moves heaven and earth for us. He orchestrates the very universe for our benefit. He tells us, "Yet in all these things we are more than conquerors through Him who loved us" (Rom. 8:37). "And we know that all things work together for good to those who love God, to those who are called according to His purpose" (Rom. 8:28). "He who did not spare His own Son, but delivered Him up for us all, how shall He not with Him also freely give us all things?" (Rom. 8:32) Jesus has restored to us all His authority in heaven and on earth, and He has made us more than conquerors in His precious name (Matt. 28:18).

Inconspicuously nestled amid the story of Joseph in the book of Genesis is the story of Tamar. Judah, one of the sons of Jacob and Leah, chose a wife, Tamar, for his firstborn son, Er. Er was such a wicked man that the Lord killed him. Judah then told his second born son to take Tamar to wife and produce an heir in his brother's name. But Onan knew the heir would not be his, so when he slept with Tamar, he dumped his seed onto the ground so she could not conceive. This greatly displeased the Lord, so he killed Onan as well. Then Judah instructed Tamar to stay in his home as a widow, and when his youngest son, Shelah, was grown, Judah would give Tamar to him as his wife.

Time passed, Shelah grew up, but Judah did not give him to Tamar as a husband. Judah's wife had died as well; therefore, he was a widower, but he did not offer to take Tamar as his wife, either. Her biological clock was ticking out, and the men who were supposed to do right by her were not. She had kept her end of the bargain and lived as a widow in Judah's house many years, but Judah was not keeping his word to Tamar, nor abiding by the requirements of the law. Tamar had wasted her prime years just waiting.

One day, it was told to Tamar that her father-in-law was going up to Timnah to shear sheep. So she took off her widow's weeds, covered herself with a veil, and then sat in an open place that was on the way to Timnah. When Judah saw her, he thought she was a harlot because she had covered her face. He entreated her to sleep with him, and she asked, "What have you to give me, that you may come in to me?" (Gen. 38:16) He suggested that he could send her a young goat from his flocks. She responded that would be fine but asked him what he would leave her as a pledge until he could fulfill his end of the bargain. He asked what she might require. She responded, "Your signet and cord, and your staff that is in your hand" (Gen. 38:18). Judah gave her the articles she requested, and then he slept with her.

Miraculously, God blessed her, and she conceived. Even more amazing, He gave her a double blessing because she was carrying twins. She returned to Judah's house and again donned her widow's garments. After about three months, it became evident that Tamar was pregnant. When Judah heard, he was irate, and he yelled to his servants to drag her out of the house to be burned. Before they seized her, she grabbed all the articles that she had received from Judah, and when the servants threw her at Judah's feet, Tamar proclaimed, "By the man to whom these belong, I am with child" (Gen. 38: 25). Judah acknowledged that the signet, cord, and staff were his, and he replied, "She has been more righteous than I, because I did not give her to Shelah my son" (Gen. 38:26).

At the appointed time, Tamar delivered two healthy baby boys. As she was giving birth, one boy put his hand out and the midwife tied a scarlet thread to his finger, then he withdrew his hand and the other twin came out first. They named the firstborn Perez, which means "to break through," and the second twin they called Zerah, which means "a rising of light." Perez was the great-great-great-great-grandfather of Boaz, and Boaz was the great-grandfather of King David; therefore, Perez is listed in the line of Christ. Tamar refused to be a victim, and she took steps to pursue her heart's desire, and God blessed her beyond what she could think or ask.

Tamar means "to stand erect" or it means palm tree. Tamar could have accepted the unrighteous behavior that her father-in-law committed against her as her lot in life and resigned herself to being a childless widow, but she didn't. She knew that was not God's heart for her life. She knew that under the law God had granted her certain rights, namely another husband and a child. Although her steps were drastic, she was determined to change her stars. She was not content to sit back like a helpless victim and let what man meant for evil against her to just happen. God wants to bless us and help us, but it is a whole lot easier for him to bless a moving target than one holed up in fetal position completely overwhelmed by helplessness and depression. Tamar stood tall, she contrived a plan, and she moved forward in faith.

In her loneliness, perhaps God spoke to her through the Scriptures. Perhaps she was armed with Jeremiah 20:11, "But the Lord is with me as a mighty awesome one. Therefore, my persecutors will stumble and will not prevail." Maybe she clung to Isaiah 48:17, "I am the Lord your God, who teaches you to profit, who leads you by the way you should go." Or maybe she was firmly rooted in Psalms 37:23, "The steps of a good man are ordered by the Lord, and He delights in His way. Though he fall, he shall not be cast down; For the Lord upholds him with His hand."

What we do know is that Tamar steeled her nerves and took bold steps to secure what she knew the Lord wanted her to have. Like a tall, graceful palm tree, she was blown over sideways by negative circumstances, but she did not let those circumstances break her or defeat her. She remained rooted in her belief that her God would supply her need. It took a little ingenuity on her part, but once she realized that these men were not going to do right by her, she helped them to do the righteous thing.

As helpmeets, that is what we do—we actively help our loved ones to do the right thing. We gently guide and direct and give counsel when we see a need. We intervene when circumstances require. I remember one time, as a very young woman, I announced to my mother that I was going to live with a man before we got married. She adamantly told me in no uncertain terms that I was I not going to do that, that that behavior was not allowed in our family nor will it ever be, and that was that! She spoke so forcefully that I wouldn't have thought for a second to disobey her wishes. Matter of fact, her tone was so sure and certain, and felt so morally correct, that I was ashamed that I had entertained the thought. Her words spoke truth to my spirit, and I knew she was right. Never again did I entertain that thought! As helpmeets and comforters, we speak God's truths, wisdom, and life into the lives of our loved ones.

Sometimes, like Tamar and my mother, we must practice tough love. If a loved one is about to do something foolish, we do everything in our power to prevent it. If a loved one is being disrespectful, mean, or rude, then we lovingly correct by teaching the importance of kindness. If loving correction is ignored and meanness turns into abuse or violence, then often we remove ourselves from the relationship. As His precious shekinahs, we are His beloved princesses, His most beloved daughters, and He wants us to know that He imparts to us His wisdom, His knowledge, His power, and His grace. When we seek His guidance, He makes us more than conquerors and gives us victory over every aspect of our lives. We have His heart, His attention, and His assurance that He is working every negative situation in our lives to our good. Our part, like Tamar, is to believe Him, to seek His wisdom, and then to muster the courage to reach for the stars.

Blessed is the woman who puts her hope in the Lord and blessed is the woman who knows God's heart of love toward her. In 1 John 14:7, Scripture says, "If you had known Me, you would have known My Father also; and from now on you know Him and have seen Him." Old Testament stories point forward to Christ, and the New Testament reveals God's heart toward His beloved. Whatever Jesus did then, He does now because He is the same yesterday, today, and forever (Heb. 13:8). Jesus is our Deliverer, our Healer, our Provider, our Savior, our Protector and our Friend, our Victory *now*! With Him, nothing is impossible (Luke 1:37).

Do you have a need? Ask! James says, "You have not, because you ask not" (James 4:2). What are the secret desires of your heart? Ask! Psalms says, "Ask of me and I will give you the nations" (Ps. 2:8). God wants to give you the secret petitions of your heart and He is saying, "Move forward in faith!" He is bigger than all the obstacles that you can name that are standing in the way. If it is important to you, He will help you make it happen. Do not settle for the status quo or second best. Go for the brass ring. Move forward in faith and watch God bless. Jeremiah says, "Call to Me, and I will answer you, and show you great and mighty things, which you do not know" (Jer. 33:3). If He parted the Red Sea for the Israelites, He can do it again for you. Mark wrote:

> For assuredly, I say to you, whoever says to this mountain, "Be removed and be cast into the sea," and does not doubt in his heart, but believes that those things he says will be done, he will have whatever he says. Therefore I say to you, whatever things you ask when you pray, believe that you receive them, and you will have them. (Mark 11:23–24)

Like Tamar, with Christ we can change our stars. Our part is to bring our petitions before the Lord and ask. When we know beyond know who we are in Christ and believe His great love for us, then we know without a shadow of doubt that He is for us and He is working all things out for our good. We can hold our heads high, brimming over with confidence, because we have His assurance that He is guiding our steps and He will cause us to come out on top. We have His word that our persecutors shall not prevail, that He will cause them to stumble and supernaturally thwart their plans. We are His beloved, and just as Jesus is right now, exalted and lifted up, so are we (1 John 4:17). God's heart is to lavish on us all the blessings that He desires to lavish on His Son. What a glorious blessing that because of Christ's finished work on the cross, I will never again get what I deserve. Thanks to His great love, I get only what Jesus deserves! As his precious daughters, we are so divinely blessed!

Revelation

Once I believed I deserved disease, depression, punishment, and judgment, but now I know, thanks to Christ's finished work on the cross, I don't get what I deserve—I get what Jesus deserves.

Prayer of Praise

Thank You, Lord, for Your tender, loving mercies and kindnesses that hunt me down. Thank You, Lord, that Your grace and forgiveness are infinitely greater than my sins and failures. Thank You, Jesus, that my salvation does not depend on my merit but Yours. Thank You that it is Your virtue, Your goodness, and Your holiness that represents me before God. Thank You that You take every negative circumstance, even those I have caused, and You turn it to good for those who love You. Thank You that You have great plans to prosper me, Lord, and to grant me my heart's desires. In You I am more than a conqueror, and I shall see victory on all sides.

Rahab: Daring, Discerning and Delivered

It is a fearsome thing to stand before the Holy God of the Old Testament. The God of Israel: turned water to blood, sent swarms of locusts, flies, and frogs to plague the land, parted the Red Sea, raised the dead to life, stopped the sun in the sky, and brought down formidable cities with just a shout. Israel's holy God fought for His people, blessed them when they obeyed Him, cursed them when they disobeyed, and when He come down to Mt. Sinai with lightning, thundering, and smoking like a furnace, it struck terror in the hearts of His people. All who came into His presence did so with much fear and trembling.

For Christians like me who got stuck underneath the yoke of the law, we lived in constant fear of incurring God's wrath and displeasure. For those of us who didn't understand all that we inherited under grace, but instead placed our faith in the wrong covenant, we have spent years trapped in a vicious cycle of condemnation and defeat due to wrong thinking. We got massively mixed up trying to walk in both covenants. We got saved under the language of His marvelous grace, but then incorrect preaching brought us back under the judgment of the law.

To be saved, and then to revert back to old covenant thinking is a recipe for misery. Not only does it make all the blessing of the cross null and void, it causes the worst kind of hopelessness, discouragement, depression, and despair. Grace gives us a glimpse of His glory, divine mercy, and love, but then the law disqualifies us from receiving it. Grace gives us the hope of heaven and eternal life, but then the law makes us feel unworthy, undeserving, and robs us of the prize. It is the cruelest state to be saved by grace yet live under the law. It is the worst kind of deception and Satan's greatest weapon for disarming us of the power and authority found in the cross.

Under grace, we are heirs to everything Jesus gets and deserves, but under the law, we get what we deserve. Under grace, we are made daughters of the Most High, but under the law, we are made slaves to sin. There is no mixing of the two covenants; you are either saved unto life and every good and perfect gift from the Father, or you are under the law and you deserve the full penalty of the law's demands.

Joseph Prince tells a story of a woman who worked as a housekeeper for a very rich man. She served him faithfully many years until he died. He left her a letter, which she put in a frame and hung up on her wall as a remembrance of him. Unfortunately, she did not know how to read, so she never knew what his final words were. Many years passed and the woman grew very poor. Due to her advanced age, she couldn't find another secure position. She only barely scraped together enough work to keep herself fed.

One day, a young neighbor stopped by to visit. As they were enjoying a cup of tea, the neighbor noticed the piece of paper displayed on the old woman's otherwise barren walls. As the neighbor was reading it out loud, she realized that this was the last will and testament of someone. The neighbor asked her friend, "Who gave you this?" The old woman replied, "He was my employer for many years." The neighbor responded, "Did you know that he had no heirs and he has named you as the beneficiary of all that he owned?" The old woman shamefully admitted that she could not read, so she never knew what his final sentiments were. The neighbor exclaimed, "You are an heiress to a vast fortune! Everything this man owned has been yours since the day he died!"

Dumbfounded and stupefied, the old woman could only shake her head in a mixture of awe, disbelief, and then soul-sickening regret. With tears running down her deeply distraught face, she remorsefully lamented, "All these years I have suffered, done without, and just barely survived when actually I have been the heiress of a vast estate and great fortune. What a waste! What a foolish, foolish waste! I could have been living as a princess, instead of like this, a pathetic pauper. All because I didn't know! I didn't know!"

Tragically, this story mirrors the first forty years of my Christian walk with the Lord. I got saved at sixteen. I was full of His Spirit and enthusiasm for the things of the Lord. I was a baby Christian with no understanding, but I knew Jesus had entered my heart and I was filled with great awe and wonderment that Jesus had saved me from my sins and that I now had the hope of heaven. Then I started going to church. Little by little, I was fed the law, and little by little, I began to think that God was not pleased with me, that I wasn't righteous enough to be worthy of God's consideration or notice. For years I got trapped in the poverty of my sins and my sinful condition. Then my husband divorced me, and my poverty was complete. Surely, that sin would forever exclude me from any further blessings from God. I was sure that in His eyes, I was branded a failure, morally bankrupt, whether I wanted it or not was beside the point. In the eyes of God my marriage had failed, therefore I was guilty and condemned.

I wasted many years trapped in the poverty of my sins, feeling isolated and rejected, when actually I was 100 percent forgiven two thousand years ago. On the day I invited Jesus into my heart, I was made a blood-bought heiress of the Most High. For forty years, I missed the truth of His grace! I was ignorant of all that is mine in Christ Jesus, thanks to His finished work on the Cross. I didn't know! I didn't hear Him, and I couldn't see His words of grace for me in His word. When I did read grace verses, I disqualified myself, believing that those verses only apply to the good Christians, not the fallen ones like me.

The law had blinded me. I was just as illiterate to God's truth as the poor old housekeeper. She lived dirt poor many years, although she was an heiress to a great fortune. In the same way, I lived spiritually destitute for forty years, trapped in a dismal cycle of discouragement, depression, and defeat, although in reality, I was actually lavishly loved and provided for, an heiress to every good and perfect gift that our Heavenly Father desires to lavish on His Son.

What a blessed revelation that whereas once I lived in constant fear of incurring God's wrath and displeasure, now I know I am saved from fear, wrath, death, and hell and I am saved unto His safety, His shalom peace, His infinite love, His immeasurable grace, and every possible blessing from above! His grace removed the veil from my eyes and allowed me to finally see the truth of His word, the truth of all that I am in Christ Jesus. All praise and glory to His wonderful name by whose authority all power and grace are given unto us! All the authority and power that Jesus possesses in heaven, He imparts to us right now. His authority and power make us fearless, discerning, and delivers us to the uttermost. Praise His glorious name!

The story of Rahab is an encouraging faith picture of a woman who was daring and discerning, and it resulted in the deliverance of her whole household from destruction. Joshua, Moses's successor, sent out two spies to view the Promised Land, especially the city and area around Jericho. When the two spies entered Jericho, they lodged in an inn run by a harlot named Rahab. In no time the king of Jericho heard that two Israelites had come into his city and that they were searching out all the country to conquer it. So the king sent men to Rahab's establishment and told her to send out the two men, but Rahab had hid the spies in stalks of flax on the roof. She told the king's men that yes, they had come to her place but that they had left when it was dark. She suggested to the king's men that if they pursued them quickly, they may be able to overtake the two Israelites.

After she got all her boarders settled for the night, she went up on the roof and spoke to the two spies. She said,

> I know that the LORD has given you the land,
> that the terror of you has fallen on us, and that
> all the inhabitants of the land are faint-hearted
> because of you. For we have heard how the

LORD dried up the Red Sea for you when you came out of Egypt, and what you did to the two kings of the Amorites who were on the other side of the Jordan, Sihon, and Og, whom you utterly destroyed. And as soon as we heard these things, our hearts melted; neither did there remain any more courage in anyone because of you, for the LORD your God, He is God in heaven above and on earth beneath. Now therefore, I beg you, swear to me by the LORD, since I have shown you kindness, that you also will show kindness to my father's house, and give me a true token, and spare my father, my mother, my brothers, my sisters, and all that they have, and deliver our lives from death. (Joshua 2:9–13)

The two spies promised to spare Rahab and her family in exchange for their lives. They told her to bring her whole family into her house, to keep them there, and to hang a scarlet cord out her window. If any of her family left her house, their blood would not be on the head of Israel. Rahab let the spies down a rope from her window, for her house sat on the outer wall of the city. She told them to run to the mountains and hide there for three days until their pursuers returned to Jericho, then it would be safe to continue on their way. The spies returned to their camp at Acacia Grove and reported to Joshua all that had happened. When the Israelites attacked and destroyed Jericho with just a shout, Rahab and her family were spared. Joshua sent the two spies into Jericho to bring out Rahab, her family, and all that she had and then they burned the city.

Rahab, a harlot, saved her entire family from destruction. She had the discernment to know that her family was in imminent danger, and she had the courage to try and save them. She is a type of the Holy Spirit because she had the wisdom and spiritual discernment to sense what was going on around her. She sensed the danger, and she took steps to ensure the safety of her family. By her quick wit and expeditious thinking, she placed herself in a position of leverage. She perceived that God was moving, that she was in jeopardy, and she had the wisdom and bravery to act quickly and decisively. She was in the right place at the right time, but more importantly, she had the spiritual intuitiveness and sensitivity to understand what was happening and then sized up instantly a way around the problem. God provided her a way of escape, and Rahab was discerning and daring enough to take advantage of the opportunity.

A blood red cord became her lifeline. Just like the blood on the doorposts spared the Israelites from the scourge of the death angel, a blood red cord spared Rahab's house from destruction. God said, "When I see the blood, I will pass over you" (Exod 12:13). Why does God's wrath and judgment pass over us? It is because we are covered by the blood of Christ. When God sees a believer, He sees us wrapped in a cloak covered by the blood of Jesus. Our robes of righteousness are fashioned from Christ's virtue, His sinless perfection, and His holy, spotless blood. Not to sound gory, but life is in the blood. We have the assurance of eternal life and a righteous standing before God solely based on the blood of Jesus. He paid the penalty for our sin by cutting a new covenant on our behalf using His own righteous blood. We are saved because we are covered by His blood. The blood of Jesus is our lifeline.

Rahab eventually married Salmon of the tribe of Judah, and they bore a son named Boaz, who is the great-grandfather of David. She is listed in the line of Christ. I love the story of Rahab, because it proves there is room at the cross for me. She was a harlot, and yet she is listed in the genealogy of Jesus. She did not let the sins of her past define who she was, but she identified herself with the God of the Hebrews. In the same way, my past or my mistakes do not define me, because I identify myself with Christ. It's Jesus's righteousness that defines me, and He says He remembers my sins no more. Matter of fact, He removes them as far as the east is from the west. The good news is, there is room at the cross for all of us, because our identity is forever one with Christ Jesus, and He is our righteousness.

We do not know the circumstances that lead Rahab into such a cruel life, but I love that she felt she was worthy of saving. I love how the Bible shows that fallen people can be redeemed, that God can still use us. She wasn't tossed aside and discarded because she had lived an immoral life style; on the contrary, she was used mightily by the Lord. She not only saved the life of the two Israelite spies, she saved herself and her whole family, and she ended up the great-great-grandmother to a king. Rahab means proud. She proudly and boldly received the God of the Hebrews as her God, and proudly, she is an ancestor of the King of kings.

Jesus came to save sinners. So for those of us who have a less-than-stellar past, we can take comfort in the fact that there is room at the cross for us. The Bible is filled with people who have a colorful past. Abraham, the father of the faithful, was a coward. Twice he tried to pass his wife off as his sister when heathen kings wanted her in their harems. Jacob was a conniving cheater. He cheated his father and brother out of the birthright blessing. Saul was insanely jealous, dabbled in witchcraft, and sought to murder his successor. David was a murderer and adulterer. Solomon was lustful with an insatiable appetite for women, and Paul was a murderer. Great people can have great flaws and can make horrific mistakes, but the point is that God used these flawed specimens of humanity to accomplish His word.

The name Jesus means "the Lord our Savior." Saving us is God's job. Our part is to hear Him and believe Him. When the Philippian jailer asked Paul and Silas, "What must I do to be saved?" Paul answered, "Believe on the Lord Jesus Christ, and you will be saved, you and your household" (Acts 16:30–31). We are all flawed vessels, yet God delights in using the weak, the broken, the old, and the fallen to confound the mighty (1 Cor. 1:27). For with God, all things are possible and perfect love casts out fear (Matt. 19:26; 1 John 4:18). Like the shepherd boy David, when we believe that all things are possible with God, it gives us the courage to come against the giants in our lives. When we believe that Jesus is our Savior, then we can live boldly knowing that if He is for us, what can man do against us? Rahab believed in the God of Israel and she believed He could save her, which gave her the courage to ask. She asked, and Jesus saved.

When we put our lives in God's hands, when we hear His words and believe Him, He leads us into a place of peace, blessing, safety, and rest. He rescues us from the stains and bondages of sin and elevates us to the position of sons and daughters of the Most High. He saves us from hell and from the penalty of our sins, and He saves us unto every good and perfect gift that God the Father desires to bestow on God the Son. We receive a princess portion of blessings because we are an heiress to the wealth of the universe (Deut. 8:18; Is. 60:5; Ps. 112:3). Our part is to come boldly before the throne of grace. Like Rahab, we should be sensitive to the movement of the Holy Spirit, discerning how we might join Her to make a difference in our world, then muster the courage and daring to move forward and watch how the Lord delivers us on every level.

Like Rahab, when we put our faith and trust in our Savior, He saves us. He will not disappoint us for that which He says, He will do. He assures us, "Indeed I have spoken it; I will also bring it to pass. I have purposed it; I will also do it" (Isa. 46: 11). We never have to fear Him again, and we can have complete confidence that He is for us. For He Himself said, "I will never leave you nor forsake you. So we may boldly say, 'The LORD is my helper; I will not fear. What can man do to me?'" (Heb. 13:5–6) What a blessed revelation to finally see, hear, and understand that Jesus is my Lord and my Savior! Like Rahab, we can rejoice because Jesus saves us to the uttermost!

Revelation

Once I lived in constant fear of His wrath and displeasure, but now I know I am saved from fear, wrath, death, and hell, and I am saved unto His safety, His shalom peace, His love, and every blessing the Father desires to lavish on His Son.

Prayer of Praise

Thank you, Jesus, that there is room at the cross for me. Lord, you came to earth to save those who are lost and hopeless in their sins. Lord, I cannot undo the mistakes of my past, and I am exceedingly thankful that You forgive me right where I am at, and despite what I have done. I cry out to You, Lord, freely admitting that I am a sinner in need of Your grace, and I thank You and praise You that You receive me just as I am, warts and all! Thank You that You made a way for me, that I am free to love you with my entire heart and soul, because You first loved me with Your entire body, soul, and Spirit. You laid down Your life as my perfect sacrifice. You took the penalty for what I deserved in Your own body. You suffered immeasurable agonies to redeem me back into fellowship with my Heavenly Father. You became my righteousness so that I can stand before my Heavenly Father in all Your glory, Your power, and Your authority, not in my sin and shame. You made me a princess, a priestess, an heiress, and a beloved daughter of the Most High. My heart swells with joy when I consider all that You accomplished for me at the cross. Thank You, Jesus, with all my heart!

The Great Woman of Shunam: The Righteousness of Faith Speaks

Death and life are in the power of the tongue. The old adage "Sticks and stones may break my bones, but words can never hurt me" is so incredibly false. Words have tremendous power to hurt or to heal, as most of us can testify. From heaven's perspective, words have creative power. When God decided to launch His creation, His first words were not "Wow! It's so dark!" On the contrary, He said, "Let there be light," and there was light! He didn't speak what was—He spoke what He wanted to see, and He spoke the world into existence. Because we are made in the image of God, our words have creative power as well.

We speak into existence the things we say. We don't realize it, but so many times we speak the exact opposite of what we want. We say things like "I'm so fat," or "I'm so broke," or "I'm so tired," and we speak into our existence the opposite of what we want. If we say those negative words enough, they become our reality. Instead, we need to say things like "I am a fat burner, not a fat storer" or "The Lord is my Shepherd, I shall not lack" or "I can do all things through Christ who strengthens me." With God, words matter, and our words carry power.

So many of God's promises ask us to speak or ask. Romans 10:9 says, "If you confess with your *mouth* the Lord Jesus and believe in your heart that God raised Him from the dead, you will be saved" (emphasis mine). Joshua 1:8 records, "This Book of the Law shall not depart from your *mouth*, but you shall meditate [meaning *utter* or *mutter* under your breath] in it day and night...For then you will make your way prosperous, and then you will have good success" (emphasis mine). Notice that when we constantly utter God's promises and words, then we will make our way prosperous, and we will have good success. What makes us prosperous and successful? Speaking God's Word.

Second Corinthians 4:13 tell us, "I believed and therefore I *spoke*, we also believe and therefore *speak*." Jesus also said, "Whoever *says* to this mountain, 'Be removed and cast into the sea,' and does not doubt in his heart, but believes that those things he *says* will be done, he will have whatever he *says*" (Mark 11:23). James 4:2 says, "You have not because you *ask* not," and Psalms 2:8 tell us, "*Ask* of Me and I will give you the nations." Isaiah proclaims, "So shall My word be that goes forth from My *mouth*. It shall not return to Me void. But it shall accomplish what I please, and it shall prosper in the thing for which I sent it." (All emphasis mine.) God hears our words and gives them power, therefore what we say seriously matters.

We can choose to speak life, or we can speak death. Because we live in such a fallen, sarcastic, verbally caustic society, many of us do not even realize how much death and negativity we actually speak. We have grown up on TV programs whose sole dialogue centers around one cutting retort after another. Some people consider that comedy, but if we transfer that kind of verbal vomit to real life, then we are speaking death. As helpers and comforters, we were created to speak life into our loved ones and to those around us. As His glorious shekinahs, our presence and our conversation should bring light into a room.

When people leave our presence, our words should leave them feeling encouraged, lifted up, and affirmed. We should never miss an opportunity to say the positive things we are thinking about others. After losing my second brother, it impressed on me quite young, that we may not have tomorrow to say the encouraging, complimentary things we were thinking about a person, so speak it when it comes to mind. Share with others the things you love and appreciate about them. Whenever you can, and as much as you can, speak life into others.

As His warrior princesses, we should arm ourselves with His belt of truth, His breastplate of righteousness, His shoes that bring the gospel of peace, His helmet of salvation, and His sword of the Spirit, which is the word of God, and protect those in our sphere of influence from the fiery darts of the enemy. It can be brutal out there in the world, so it is important that our homes and our spheres of influence be a place of affirmation and encouragement. My mother was the queen of exhortation. She would say things like, "You girls are so smart, so talented, and you can do anything you put your minds to." She was always there to encourage us, to support us, and to cheer us on. She would lovingly correct us when needed, but her words always felt like cool, refreshing water over parched, dry earth.

One of my mother's favorite maxims was, "There is never an excuse to be unkind." She really was the most gracious lady I have ever met. She always chose to speak life. Even after the death of her second son to what was a preventable accident, she said to my dad, who was inadvertently responsible for both his son's deaths, "You were a good father." He knew he had made horrific mistakes, and I am sure he was riddled with soul-sickening remorse and regret, but my mother didn't cast blame or speak death—she chose to affirm him and to speak life. She truly was a remarkable shekinah!

In the book of Second Kings is an amazing faith picture of a woman who would only speak life. Whenever the prophet Elisha would pass through the town of Shunam, there was a gracious woman who would persuade Elisha to eat with her and her husband. One day, the Shunammite woman said to her husband:

> Look now, I know that this is a holy man of God, who passes by us regularly. Please let us make a small upper room on the wall; and let us put a bed for him there, and a table and a chair and a

lampstand; so it will be, whenever he comes to us
he can turn in there. (2 Kings 4:9–10)

In time, Elisha wanted to return kindness to the Shunammite
woman, but she refused to take anything for her hospitality. Elisha's
servant, Gehazi, told Elisha that the woman didn't have any children, and her husband was old. He told Gehazi to go call her. When
she came and stood in the doorway, Elisha told her that about this
time next year she shall embrace a son. She was so taken back, she
said, "No, my lord. Man of God, do not lie to your maidservant!"
(2 Kings 4:16) But the kind woman of Shunam conceived and bore
a son just as Elisha had told her.

The child grew and was an utter joy and delight to the older
couple. One day, when the boy went to join his father in the fields, he
cried, "My head, my head!" A servant carried the boy to his mother,
and at around noon, he died. She took her son upstairs and laid him
on the man of God's bed, shut the door, and then she called to her
husband to bring one of the donkeys so she could run to Elisha and
bring him back. Her husband asked, "Why are you going to him
today?" She replied, "It is well," and she left.

When the man of God saw her afar off, he sent his servant
Gehazi to go and see what she wanted. When Gehazi asked her if
all is well, she responded, "It is well," yet when she reached Elisha,
she fell at his feet and clung to him. She cried, "Did I ask a son
of my lord? Did I not say, 'Do not deceive me'?" (2 Kings 4:28)
Immediately, Elisha instructed Gehazi to run ahead and to lay his
staff on the child's face, but the child did not awaken. When Elisha
entered his room, the child was lying dead on the bed. He shut the
door and prayed to the Lord, and then he went and lay on the child.
He put his mouth on the child's mouth, his eyes on his eyes, his
hands on his hands, and he stretched himself out on the child, and
the flesh of the child became warm. Elisha got up, walked about the
room, prayed some more, and then again stretched out on top of the
child. The child sneezed seven times and then opened his eyes. Elisha

told Gehazi to go get the Shunammite woman and tell her to come up and get her son. The woman fell at the feet of the man of God, then picked up her son and left his room.

This woman is called the great woman of Shunam because of her great faith. She believed that if Elisha could give her the miracle of a son, then he could also bring her son back to life. She is a type of Holy Spirit because she fed, cared for, and lovingly provided for the man of God. Also, she spoke into existence that what she wanted to see. When her son died, she told no one. She would not say it out loud. She would only speak "It is well," and then she ran straight to the man of God and asked for a miracle. As his shekinahs, this should be our response as well. Don't speak the bad, but instead, speak what you want to see, and speak what God's word says about you and your situation. How many miracles have we missed because we gave utterance to the negative, instead of by faith, speaking what we need and then believing God for our miracles?

You will notice that the great woman of Shunam didn't seek the consolation of her husband or her friends and neighbors. She did not instantly start grieving and fall to pieces. She did not stand there in shock, frozen into inaction. Nor did she shake her fist at God in anger. She did not respond in any of the ways we normally do. This humble, selfless, generous woman is so godly because her response was godly. She knew that her God was a mighty God, and she had confidence that the man of God would restore her son.

While Jesus walked the earth, He healed the sick and lame, He chased out demons, He fed the multitudes, and He brought the dead to life. As Jesus is right now, exalted and lifted up, seated at the right hand of the Father, so are we in this world (1 John 4:17). As Jesus is given power and authority, so are we. As Jesus healed, so can we. As Jesus prayed for and received miracles, so can we. The great woman of Shunam is a faith picture to show us how to apprehend our miracles. She is called a great woman because she had great faith. Like this gracious shekinah, we are all great women in the eyes of God when we chose to speak life, when we place our confidence in our Savior, and when we bring our petitions before our Holy Man of God, believing that He hears us and that it is His heart to bless us and prosper us. Great faith believes that our loving Heavenly Father hears our requests and that our words shall not return void.

Our part under the new covenant is to hear Him, to believe Him, and to speak His word, His promises, and His faith pictures. Romans 10:6 declares, "The righteousness of faith speaks." One day, a Roman centurion came to Jesus because a servant who was very dear to him was sick and close to death. The centurion didn't want to trouble Jesus, so he asked if Jesus would just say the Word, and his servant would be healed. For the centurion was a commander of soldiers and he knew if the commanding officer gives the word, it is as good as done. When Jesus heard the centurion's faith, He marveled, for He had not seen such great faith in all of Israel (Luke 7:1–10). The centurion knew all Jesus had to do was to speak. The centurion heard about Jesus, He believed in Him, and He knew if Jesus spoke a command, it would be done.

Proverbs 4:20–27 tells us:

> My [daughters], give attention to my words; incline your ear to my sayings. Do not let them depart from your eyes; keep them in the midst of your heart; for they are life to those who find them, and health to all their flesh. Keep your heart with all diligence, for out of it spring the issues of life. Put away from you a deceitful mouth, and put perverse lips far from you. Let your eyes look straight ahead, and your eyelids look right before you. Ponder the path of your feet, and let all your ways be established. Do not turn to the right or the left; remove your foot from evil.

This passage describes those believers of great faith. They give attention to the word of God, and they hear the message spoken. They keep their eyes, mind, and heart focused on God's promises with all diligence. They do not indulge perverse thoughts or vain utterances that contradict God's word, nor speak deceitful lies that originate from the enemy of their souls, but, instead, they chose to set their eyes on the Son of God, looking upward only, planting their feet firmly on the path of His righteousness and power, establishing their faith on the Rock of our Salvation, believing that He is the source of all blessing, and choosing to speak life into their situation or circumstance.

Great faith hears Him, believes Him, and speaks His resurrection life and power into existence. God gives life to the dead. He speaks into existence everything that is dead in us to superglorious resurrection life and power. God calls those things (all my blessings, healings, and anointing) which don't yet exist, as though they did (Rom. 4:17). Know this, that the Lord your God, He is God, the faithful God who keeps His covenant and mercy for a thousand generations with those who love Him (Deut. 7:9).

Years later, the great woman of Shunam would experience another miracle from the hand of God. Elisha warned the Shunammite woman that there would be famine in the land, so she went with Elisha to the land of the Philistines and lived there for seven years. When they returned to Shunam, she had to plead with the king of Israel to get her house and lands back, which had been illegally taken by others during her absence. Her attempt to appeal to the king brought her before him on the same day that the king had requested an audience with Gehazi. The king was very interested to hear about all the miracles performed by Elisha. Gehazi told the king that waiting for an audience is a woman who could tell the king firsthand about two of Elisha's miracles.

The king was very excited to hear her report, which gave the Shunammite woman the opportunity to share the story of how Elisha not only gave her a son in her older age, but how he raised her son from the dead. The king was so pleased with her report that He listened to her appeal and restored to the Shunammite her house and lands, as well as all the proceeds from the land since the day she left. God had placed the Shunammite woman in the right place at the right time. Only a great and mighty God could orchestrate such an event, so great is His love and care for his people. We can declare with confidence, "I will say of the Lord, He is my refuge and my fortress; My God in Him will I trust" (Ps. 91:2).

Like the great woman of Shunam, we can apprehend our miracles if we hear Him, believe what He says, and speak into our existence everything He says is true about us. Faith is the substance of things hoped for, the evidence of things not seen. Faith speaks life and proclaims every promise which we don't yet see. Faith speaks that which is already ours in the eternal into our temporal. Life, superabundant, resurrected life, is in the power of the tongue and blessed and happy is the woman who chooses to speak life.

God will never be stingy or hardhearted with us. As His precious shekinahs, we are great women in the eyes of God when, like the Shunammite, we speak life, placing complete confidence in the goodness of our God and in His great love for us. He delights when we come boldly before His throne of grace, asking, speaking, and declaring our miracle healings, provisions, and restorations. Great faith knows and believes that the righteousness of faith speaks.

Revelation

Once I was harsh and critical with my words, because I felt God was harsh and critical of me, but now I know I am the righteousness of God in Christ, and my words have creative power, therefore, I choose to speak life.

Prayer of Praise

Thank You, Lord, that You give my words creative power and You promise that my words shall not come back void. Teach me, O Lord, to speak that which I want to see and to refrain from speaking negative words that do not agree with Your word. I know I cannot control the thoughts that waft in and out of my mind, but I can choose what comes out of my mouth. Thank You, Jesus, that thoughts have no power, only what I give voice to does, so teach me to speak only life. When I do have negative thoughts, teach me, O Lord, not to speak them. Throughout the day, I commit to intentionally speak Your words, Your promises, and Your faith pictures into my life. The righteousness of faith speaks, so I will speak and declare Your promises and blessings into me and my family's lives. For every blessing that Your word says is mine, I will speak it into my existence, for Your word says, "You give life to the dead and You call those things which do not exist as though they did" (Rom. 4:17). As Your glorious shekinah, I choose to speak into my existence Your word, Your promises, and Your blessings; I choose to speak life.

Esther: Promoted and Protected for a Purpose

Have you ever felt there was nothing worthwhile to wake up for? Has it ever seemed like you were just spinning your wheels, but going nowhere? Have you ever wondered why you are here, why you were born? God says He has great plans for us, amazing plans to prosper us. In Jeremiah, He tells us, "For I know the plans I have for you," declares the LORD, "plans to prosper you, and not to harm you, plans to give you hope and a future" (Jer. 29:11, NIV). Each one of us was put on the planet for a purpose. The LORD of hosts has sworn, saying, "Surely, as I have thought, so it shall come to pass, and as I have purposed, so it shall stand" (Isa. 14:24). The Lord puts in our hearts the desire to will and do. He also gives us the ability and resources to pursue our dreams and aspirations. When we step out in faith, He opens doors, puts us in the right place at the right time, and makes our paths smooth and our way prosperous. When we realize God has a purpose and plan for our lives, it gives us courage to step forward in faith and to work toward our goals and ambitions. Our dreams and desires matter to God, and if we will exercise our faith, He makes a way for us.

Upon my leaving graduate school, our nation entered the worst recession since the Great Depression. I was fifty-one, a teacher, and I couldn't find a job. Rather than twiddling my thumbs waiting, I used some of the research from my master's project to write a book. It took me several years, but the second publishing house that I submitted it to accepted me. This was nothing short of the divine providence of God. I was a rural teacher from North Pole, Alaska. I spent most of my career in a one-room schoolhouse, which basically means my curriculum vita was practically nonexistent, yet I was accepted by a major academic publishing house. I felt so miraculously blessed, and I knew that God had exalted me above my qualifications.

Rather than allowing a very expensive master's degree to produce nothing, I used my time of underemployment to pursue another dream. Several of my university professors encouraged me to write. Since all I could secure were lousy-paying sub-jobs, I felt at least by writing I was still producing, and therefore, I had a plan that generated a hope of paying back my student loans. I despise debt, and I felt heavily burdened by the inability to pay back what I had borrowed. The irritating thing was this debt wasn't even my idea.

During the horrific recession, Oregon's teachers licensing commission decided to start requiring teachers to earn master's degrees in order to keep their license. What bad timing! Thousands of teachers pouring out of hundreds of teaching colleges couldn't find work, and then the state, to which I had just moved, thrust the expense of a master's degree upon those already stuck in a dire situation. Highly skilled teachers were working at Starbucks or as teacher's aides, yet if you wanted to keep your license, you had to incur the debt to pursue a master's. It was such a discouraging, dismal time for me. I was so frustrated that I did not even attend my graduation ceremony.

It was during this especially bleak time that my eyes were opened to His Grace. I learned that God is not limited in any way and He provides for His own even when the economy is bad. Once I started claiming my blessings in the Lord rather than complaining, God extended incredible mercy toward me and unleashed His goodness. Not only did I get published, but He also provided me a princess assignment working as a private tutor. God delights in taking our negative circumstances and turning them into good. When we place our faith and trust in His great love and care for us, He opens the storehouses of His great and glorious blessings upon us. God, indeed, has an amazing plan and purpose for each of our lives and our part is to step forward in faith, believe what He says, and reach for the stars.

The story of Esther is an inspiring faith picture of how God has a plan to promote us and protects us for a purpose. Esther was an orphan who lived with her cousin Mordecai. Their parents, Jewish exiles, had been taken into captivity by Nebuchadnezzar, king of Babylon. Years later, when King Cyrus gave the decree that the Jews could return to their homeland, very few returned. Esther stayed in the Persian capital of Susa to remain under the protection of her cousin, who was a low-ranking official for King Xerxes.

The book of Esther opens with Xerxes divorcing his wife, Vashti, because she had refused to come to him when summoned. Xerxes's councilors thought this act of rebellion by the queen could stir wives across the kingdom to disobey their husbands, so they counseled the king to divorce her. When the king began to regret deposing Vashti, his counselors decided to hold a beauty contest for the king. Beautiful maidens from all across the kingdom were summoned to compete for the king's affection and the privilege of being selected as the next queen. When Mordecai heard of the contest, he entered his beautiful cousin, Esther.

Mordecai took her to the palace and entrusted her to the king's chief eunuch, Hegai. Esther earned the affection of Hegai because she deferred to the chief eunuch's advice on how to prepare for her audience with the king. Under Hegai's guidance, Esther found favor in the sight of all who saw her, including the king. King Xerxes loved Esther more than all the other women, so he set the royal crown upon her head.

Shortly, thereafter, Mordecai overheard a plot by two of the king's eunuchs to take the king's life. Mordecai told Esther, who told the king, and when the plot was confirmed, the two conspirators were hanged. The incident was recorded in the king's chronicles, but the incident was quickly forgotten.

Later the king promoted a man named Haman to position of prime minister, and the king commanded that all his servants should bow to Haman and pay homage to him. Mordecai would neither bow nor pay homage to Haman, because he was a descendant of one of the Hebrews' ancient enemies, the Amalekites. This infuriated Haman, and when he found out that Mordecai was a Jew, he was determined to destroy Mordecai and all the Jewish exiles. Haman tricked the king into signing a decree that issued an order that gave Persians the right to pillage and exterminate Jews throughout the entire Persian Empire. On a prescribed day stated in the decree, Haman hoped to not only annihilate the Jews but to get rich off all their possessions.

When Mordecai got word of Haman's scheme, he tore his robes and put on ashes and sackcloth. He sent word to Ester informing her that she should not think that she was safe just because she was in the palace. "When Haman finds out you are a Jewess, he will have you killed too," warned Mordecai. Esther asked the Jews in her city to fast and pray with her for three days before she requested an audience with the king. According to Persian law, upon pain of death, Esther could not approach the king unless she was summoned. Even so, after three days of fasting and prayer, Esther dressed in her finest royal robes and waited outside his throne room. When the king saw her, he was pleased, and he invited her into his presence.

When the king asked what her request was, she invited the king and Haman to a banquet that she had prepared. At the banquet, the king again asked what Esther's petition was, assuring her that whatever she wanted up to half the kingdom would be hers. She requested that the king and Haman come to a banquet in their honor again the next day. Haman was utterly delighted that he had found favor in the eyes of the king and queen.

That night, the king could not sleep, so he read through the various accounts recorded in the royal chronicles. He read that Mordecai had saved his life, and he asked his servants what honor or dignity had been bestowed on Mordecai for his act of loyalty and kindness. His servants said, "Nothing has been done for him"

(Esther 6:3). The king asked who was in the court right now. The servants told him that Haman had just arrived, for he was going to suggest to the king that they hang Mordecai on the gallows he had built just outside the castle walls.

The king asked Haman, "What shall be done for the man whom the king delights to honor?" Now Haman thought the king was referring to him. Haman answered the king:

> Let a royal robe be brought which the King has worn, and a horse on which the King has ridden, which has a royal crest placed on its head. Then let this robe and horse be delivered to the hand of one of the king's most noble princes that he may array the man whom the king delights to honor. Then parade him on horseback through the city square, and proclaim before him: "Thus shall it be done to the man whom the king delights to honor!" (Esther 6:8-9)

Then the king commanded Haman to carry out exactly the things he had suggested, and to honor Mordecai the Jew who sits at the king's gate. Haman did as he was told, but then he had to leave to attend Esther's banquet.

At the banquet, again the king asked what Esther's request was. This time the queen answered:

> If I have found favor in your sight, O king, and if it pleases the king, let my life be given me at my petition, and my people at my request. For we have been sold, my people and I, to be destroyed, to be killed, and to be annihilated. Had we been sold as male and female slaves, I would have held my tongue, although the enemy could never compensate for the king's loss. (Esther 7:3–4)

The king asked, "Who is he, and where is he, who would dare presume in his heart to do such a thing?" (Esther 7:5)

And Esther answered, "The adversary and enemy is this wicked Haman!" (Esther 7:6)

The king then ordered Haman and all his family to be hanged on the gallows that Haman had built for Mordecai. The king then promoted Mordecai to the position of prime minister, and he issued a new decree giving the Jews permission to defend themselves against their attackers on the day of the assault. Under Persian law, the king could not annul a decree, so he could not cancel the intention to commit evil against the Jews, but he could give them the authority to fight and to aid them in defending their lives and property.

The Jews thoroughly destroyed their attackers, and from that day forward, they would celebrate their deliverance from Haman's wicked plan through a new annual feast they call Purim. The king also gave Esther Haman's house, which she in turn appointed Mordecai to be the head of. What man meant for evil against Mordecai, Esther, and their people, God turned to good. God promoted Esther for a purpose, and she was able to protect herself and her people from great harm.

Esther is a type of Holy Spirit. She does not promote herself; Mordecai is the one who entered her in the competition for queen. She humbled herself and sought the advice of the one who would know the king best. Hegai is the one who told her what to wear and how to fix her hair and make-up. She asks for her people to fast and pray for three days before she would approach the king. She was willing to lay down her life to help her people. She prayed for wisdom on how to deal with Haman. She patiently waited on the Lord's leading on what to do and say and when and how to say it. Then God orchestrated all the events that led to the exposure and demise of Haman and the promotion of Esther, Mordecai, and their people.

The story of Esther teaches us that God is bigger than our problems. He responds to our prayers and fasting. He has a plan and a purpose for each of our lives—plans to prosper us and to give us hope and a future. What are the secret petitions of your heart? Are you living at your full potential and pursuing your dreams? It is God who gives us talents, gifts, creativity, ambition, and those secret desires, and He is saying, "Go for it!" Do not let fear or the overwhelming size of your dream stop you. Remember, God said that if you say to this mountain "Be moved" and do not doubt, then it has to move. We call trials, tribulations, problems, impediments, and various challenges "mountains" because mountains look and seem permanent, but they are not. If we command those mountains to melt like wax in the presence of the Lord, then, they must melt. God delights in moving our mountains, so that He gets the glory, and we get to accomplish our dreams. Mountains may not move in a day, or a month, or even this year, but be assured, if you are praying and believing, then God is working on the mountain and ultimately, it has to move.

Once I believed God was against me, but after He opened my eyes to His grace, I could see from Scriptures that He is irrevocably for me. God tells us, "Fear not, for I am with you; be not dismayed, for I am your God. I will strengthen you, I will uphold you with My righteous right hand" (Isa. 41:10). We can say with confidence, "Ah Lord God! Behold, You have made the heavens and the earth by Your great power and outstretched arm. There is nothing too hard for You" (Jer. 32:17).

Psalm 91 tells us, "A thousand may fall at your side, and ten thousand at your right hand; but it shall not come near you" (Ps. 91:7). God tells us that under His new covenant, He has given a command to bless us and it cannot be reversed (Num. 23:19–20, Heb. 6:20). God's job under the new covenant is to save us, to bless us, to heal us, to protect us, to promote us, and to provide for us. Our job is to hear Him, to receive Him, to believe Him, to speak His word and promises, and to ask.

I once felt that I did not matter to God, that He didn't even notice me. Under this oppression, I lost my way and my direction, because if God was against me and I am nowhere on His radar, then why try, or why care? Once my eyes were opened to the truth of His infinite and intimate love for me, my whole world, my total being, and my entire countenance changed. Now as I read the words He meant for me, my heart burns within me because I am so overwhelmed by His goodness. I could look back on my life and see His hand of providence at every turn. I started seeing His intimate love and care for me in every aspect of my life. I heard His voice in the words Mordecai said to Esther, "Yet who knows whether you have come to the kingdom for such a time as this?" (Esther 4:14) I put my name in every one of His promises, as if every word was a personal love letter to me. What a blessed revelation when I finally understood that my life matters to Him and that He is irrevocably for me!

About a year ago, my job required that I travel to Sicily. I am not the bravest of souls and I was really nervous about traveling internationally by myself. I said a simple prayer, "Lord, give me the courage to do this." Within days, my twin sister offered to go with me. It was a trying trip—food poisoning, no sleep due to mosquitos, and our flights were cancelled in Rome on the journey home. What should have been a twenty-eight-hour flight home ended up a forty-eight-hour exhausting ordeal! The Lord knew ahead of time all the challenges I would have to face, ones that would have utterly unnerved me had my sister not been with me. That is how intimately He loves me. He provided support, companionship, and protection in what could have been a very scary situation for me. That experience unleashed a monumental revelation; I realized that God not only loves me infinitely, but intimately as well.

If it worries me, He cares. If I am feeling anxious, He notices. If it matters to me, it matters to Him. My concerns may be nothing that concerns the next person, but if it concerns me, it concerns Him. Some people love adventure, and they are ready to go in a heartbeat. My twin sister is one of them. Her husband has said before, "We are going to Poland tomorrow," and she replied, "Awesome!" She can be packed for a two-week trip in an hour and just take a carry-on. I admire that kind of spontaneity and economy, but I have never been one of those people. I need a heads-up. I need to think about it awhile, and then I need time to plan and prepare, and I could never do a two-week trip in just a carry-on. The truth is, I do not particularly enjoy traveling; I prefer the familiarity of my own home and routines. God sees and knows all my foibles, and even though something may be no big deal to someone else, if it is a big deal to me, He cares.

We are His precious shekinahs, and He intimately cares for each of us. He knows our weakness, but He assures us when we are weak, He is strong. He knows our idiosyncrasies, and He says we are fearfully and wonderfully made. He sees us as individually unique amongst the millions, and He says He will bless us and make our name great. He sees our financial needs, and He says He will bless all the works of our hands and make all our gifts precious stones that prosper us. He sees when we are sick, and He says by His stripes we have been healed. He knows the secret petitions of our heart, and He says it is His greatest pleasure to grant us our heart's desires.

God tells us when we delight in Jesus, our Heavenly Father delights in us and showers us with every good and perfect gift from above. He says that each time we speak to our Rock of Salvation, rivers of blessing burst forth over our lives. Like the Israelites after they left Egypt, He rains down on us heavenly provisions, and He supernaturally preserves all that belongs to us so that nothing shall grow old or wear out. Everything in our lives is sustained and maintained by His resurrection life and power. He prospers us, promotes us, and protects us. How it thrills my heart to see the myriad of ways God manifests His pure, unadulterated grace, His shekinah glory, His great and mighty Presence, and His wonder-working power on all those who call upon the name of Jesus! How empowering—how awe-inspiring—to know that God is for me, to know that His universe is on my side, and that with Jesus all things are possible!

Revelation

Once I believed God was against me, but now I know He is irrevocably for me.

Prayer of Praise:

Thank You, Jesus, that as Your beloved daughter, You exalt me to the position of heavenly princess. You have predestined and infused my life with purpose. You gave me a unique set of gifts and talents to use that will bring glory to You and Your kingdom. You placed in my heart desires and ambitions that You want me to pursue. You have great plans for me—plans to prosper me and to give me hope and a future. Teach me, O Lord, to walk forward in faith and to fulfill the purpose and plans you have for me. I trust in Your great love for me, and I thank You ahead of time for all that You are about to do.

Abigail: Exhorts to a Higher Calling

Have you ever found yourself in an absolutely unbearable situation or circumstance? For some, heartbreaking circumstances began in childhood. Few people actually make it to adulthood without bearing some scars from our fallen humanity. For many of us, bad choices lead to challenging circumstances, ones in which we may not be able to extricate ourselves, but must learn to somehow live with and endure. Many of us have found ourselves in challenging relationships, ones that only persevere due to Christian commitment.

Many of us have forsaken our marriage vows when an unbearable relationship remains too unbearable for too long. Blessed are those couples who marry young and who are able to persevere through the ups and downs of marriage. There has to be very special rewards in heaven for those steadfast, committed souls who figure out how to keep a marriage healthy and strong for a lifetime. I wish I could say I was one of them, but I am not. To all the couples who have succeeded at staying in love and keeping their marriage vows, I know God says, "Well done, my faithful ones!" It is always such a privilege, an honor, and delight to observe in these happy, successful couples—humanity at its best.

In the first book of Samuel is an encouraging faith picture of a sagacious, godly woman, Abigail, who was stuck in an unbearable marriage to a brute named Nabal. During the years when David was running from the wrath of King Saul, he and his band of men were camped in the wilderness of Paran. Nabal, who was very rich, ran lots of sheep and goats near the area where David was encamped. David and his men protected Nabal's sheep herders and their flocks, and no one dared harm anything of Nabal's as long as David's army was in the vicinity. At shearing time, David sent a few of his men to Nabal to ask if he would share some of his harvest feast with David's army in exchange for his protection. Nabal reviled David's men and told them he wasn't going to give them a thing. When David heard that Nabal had returned his goodness for evil, he was furious. David ordered his men to gird their swords, and he swore he would not leave a male of Nabal's house alive.

In the meantime, one of Abigail's men had told her that David's men had come to see her husband and had asked for a small tribute, which Nabal had vehemently denied. Her servant verified that David's men were very good to them, and they did not take anything for themselves; matter of fact, they were a wall of defense for all that Nabal owned. Her servant feared imminent reprisal because of Nabal's disrespectful, churlish behavior. Abigail hastily prepared two hundred loaves of bread, two skins of wine, five sheep fully dressed, one hundred clusters of raisins, and two hundred cakes of figs and loaded them on donkeys. She and her servants set off to meet David, but she did not tell her husband.

Now when Abigail saw David, she dismounted quickly and fell on her face before him and said, "On me, my lord, on me let this iniquity be! Pay no attention to my wretched husband for he is a fool by name and a fool by nature." She told David that she did not see the men that David had sent or she would have sent her gifts then. She asked David:

> Please forgive the trespass of your maidservant.
> For the LORD will certainly make for my lord
> an enduring house, because my lord fights the
> battles of the LORD, and evil is not found in
> you throughout your days. Yet a man has risen to
> pursue you and seek your life, but the life of my

lord shall be bound in the bundle of the living with the LORD your God; and the lives of your enemies He shall sling out, as from the pocket of a sling. And it shall come to pass, when the LORD has done for my lord according to all the good that He has spoken concerning you, and has appointed you ruler over Israel, that this will be no grief to you, nor offense of heart to my lord, either that you have shed blood without cause, or that my lord has avenged himself. But when the LORD has dealt well with my lord, then remember your maidservant. (1 Samuel 25:28–31)

Then David said to Abigail,

Blessed is the LORD God of Israel, who sent you this day to meet me! And blessed is your advice and blessed are you, because you have kept me this day from coming to bloodshed and from avenging myself with my own hand. For indeed, as the LORD God of Israel lives, who has kept me back from hurting you, unless you had hurried and come to meet me, surely by morning light no males would have been left to Nabal! (1 Samuel 25:32–34)

David took the gifts Abigail had brought, and they both departed. When Abigail got home, Nabal was holding a feast and was very drunk, so she didn't tell him what had transpired that day. The following morning, when he was sober, she related all the events, mentioning how close they had come to being annihilated. Upon hearing Abigail's report, Nabal had a heart attack and then died ten days later. When David heard that Nabal had died, he said, "Blessed be the Lord, who has pleaded the cause of my reproach from the hand of Nabal, and has kept His servant from evil. For the Lord has returned the wickedness of Nabal on his own head" (1 Sam. 25:39). David then proposed to Abigail, and she became his wife.

The Bible says that Abigail was a woman of good understanding and that she was very beautiful, while Nabal her husband was harsh, cruel, selfish, rude, and evil. She was obviously a gracious, lovely woman stuck in an especially difficult marriage. How many times do we see this? A beautiful, lovely Christian woman gets unequally yoked with a harsh, selfish, mean man. I think it is wonderful that even after who knows how many years of marriage to a brute, Abigail had a beautiful countenance. She did not let the negative circumstance of her unrewarding marriage destroy her joy. Abigail means "father (or source) of joy," Obviously, if she had a glowing countenance, the source of her joy must have been her God. Isn't it amazing that although she was yoked to an angry bully, it did not affect her joy? This is why she is considered a woman of great understanding and wisdom.

Looking back on the failure of my own marriage, I can see the immaturity of my faith. Unlike Abigail, I let the circumstance of my marriage darken my countenance. I could not separate myself from my circumstance and look to the Lord as my source of joy. In those days, I did not understand His grace. I didn't believe I was loved by God, so I had no grace to love. I felt He was harsh and critical with me, so I was harsh and critical of others. At the time, I complained to God that my husband was so dysfunctional and wounded, when in retrospect, I was completely dysfunctional in my thinking about God, which made me the queen of woundedness as well. Unlike Abigail, my understanding and wisdom in the things of the Lord was zero, even though I had been saved many years.

This is why I love the story of Abigail. She is a type of the Holy Spirit, a beautiful shekinah. Her source of joy was her God. She did not let the negative things about her marriage discourage her. She did not let her husband's nastiness diminish who she was. What a feat! Her own soul, as she spoke to David, "was bound in the bundle of the living with the Lord her God." Only God can give the kind of wisdom and understanding that Abigail possessed. She did not see the mountain of her trials as permanent, and she didn't let those mountains of tribulation talk to her, rule her, or depress her. She was able to live above her mountains and trusted that God was able and willing to deal with her problems.

When her husband was set on cheating David, she quietly set out to make it right. She didn't cave in to her husband's sin and enable it; she took steps to correct it. She held the high ground, as he took the low. Like Tamar, she refused to be a victim; she was determined to do whatever virtue required. She was strong, capable, and courageous. Abigail teaches us that when we have wisdom to impart, faith to share, or help we can offer, we should be willing to run the risks or suffer the consequences to do the right thing whenever we are able. I am sure that Abigail was an expert at running to make amends and mediating for her intemperate, greedy husband. She risked enduring his brutish wrath and drunken rages to make right his mistakes if it was in her power to do so.

Abigail won David's adoration and forgiveness through her soothing, kind, wise words. She quenched his fiery indignation through a persuasive entreaty that exhorted David to hold fast to his higher calling. She kept him from shedding blood in anger, taking his own revenge, and tarnishing his godly reputation. Up until this event, he had conducted himself righteously before his God. In his rage, David was bent on murder, and Abigail knew that this really was not his character. She reminded David that no evil had been found in him all his days. She reminded him of his divine appointment as future king. Thanks to her words of exhortation, she prevented David from making a huge mistake.

Like a glorious shekinah, Abigail knew her safety and protection was from God. Maybe David wrote Psalm 91 partly for Abigail, because He certainly delivered her in a mighty way. We should all memorize this beautiful prayer of protection:

> He who dwells in the secret place of the Most High
> shall abide under the shadow of the Almighty.

I will say of the LORD, "He is my refuge and my fortress; My God, in Him I will trust."

Surely He shall deliver you from the snare of the fowler and from the perilous pestilence.

He shall cover you with His feathers, and under His wings you shall take refuge; His truth shall be your shield and buckler.

You shall not be afraid of the terror by night, nor of the arrow that flies by day, nor of the pestilence that walks in darkness, nor of the destruction that lays waste at noonday.

A thousand may fall at your side, and ten thousand at your right hand, but it shall not come near you. Only with your eyes shall you look, and see the reward of the wicked.

Because you have made the LORD, who is my refuge, even the Most High, your dwelling place, no evil shall befall you, nor shall any plague come near your dwelling; For He shall give His angels charge over you, to keep you in all your ways. In their hands they shall bear you up, lest you dash your foot against a stone…

Because he has set his love upon Me, therefore I will deliver him; I will set him on high, because he has known My name. He shall call upon Me, and I will answer him; I will be with him in trouble; I will deliver him and honor him. With long life I will satisfy him, and show him My salvation. (Psalm 91)

Abigail undoubtedly learned how to dwell in the secret place of the Most High under the shadow of His Almighty wings. In the Old Testament, God met and spoke with His people in the holy of holies in the place above the mercy seat and under the wings of the cherubim (Exod. 25:22). This is also where His Shekinah glory shone and resided when She entered the Temple. This secret place is above the mercy seat. The Bible calls Jesus our mercy seat because His blood covers every aspect of our sin and rebellion. Therefore, even when we make poor choices, like becoming unequally yoked to an ungodly man, Jesus covers our sin and rebellion and becomes our mercy seat. Abigail chose to dwell in the secret place of the Most High, which is above our sins and negative circumstances. She gloried in the Lord's presence and hid herself under His protective wings. She trusted God to be her defense, her shield, and her refuge. Her countenance radiated that she had seen His salvation. God delivered Abigail, set her on high, and greatly honored her by giving her a handsome, kind husband, who was chosen by God to be the next king of Israel.

Like the Holy Spirit, Abigail was a helper, a protector, and a peacemaker. She learned well how to help quench the flames of her husband's fiery outbursts. She remained a loyal wife and faithful protector of a worthless partner. As wretched as her life with him must have been, Abigail manifested a sacrificial love stronger than death. We have all witnessed this kind of tenacity in a few Christian women that we know—women who cling faithfully to an unworthy man because they made a covenant with God, and through sheer grit and determination, they honor their marriage vows.

I have also witnessed husbands who have turned their lives around, thanks to the prayerful perseverance of their godly wives. For our modern-day Abigails, please know you are counted among God's heroines, and I pray that you will see your day of deliverance soon. As Abigail testified, when our lives are bound in the bundle of our living Lord God, the lives of our enemies shall be slung out as from the pocket of a sling, and because He has set His love upon us, He will deliver us.

As His beloved shekinahs, we can have confidence in His great love and care for us. He sees our sufferings, and if we are praying and asking, then we can be assured that God is working on our deliverance. When we pray, He sends legions of angels to our rescue, and in their mighty hands, they bear us up. God is not slack concerning His promises, but our part is to not give up, either, but to continue to declare and speak those things He has promised us. He promises us that He is faithful, and He will not allow us to be tempted beyond what we can bear, but with each temptation, He makes a way of escape (1 Cor. 10:13). It might look bad, feel bad, and be bad, but with God, we have His promise that it will not stay bad. Like Abigail, He will deliver us and bless us mightily, because we are His beautiful shekinahs. Because we adore Him, He keeps us in the secret place of the Most High underneath the shadow of His Almighty protective wings, where we are intimately loved, infinitely adored, divinely protected, and lavishly provided for.

Revelation

Once I believed my obligation was to love God with all my heart, all my soul, and all my mind (which I failed at continually), but now I know, herein is love, not that we love Him, but that He loved us.

Prayer of Praise

Thank You, Jesus, that my response to love You naturally results from Your amazing gift of love for me. You laid down Your life for me, and took in Your own body the punishment for everything I deserved. No greater love has any man than this, than One Who would lay down His life for another. You took everything I deserved, then gave me everything You deserve. Your amazing love exhorts me to live in a way that brings honor to Your sacrificial gift. Thank You, Lord, that I can live and love from a position of hope, blessing, and victory, thanks to all that You accomplished for me at Calvary. Thank You, that my life and my worth is bound up in the bundle of my living Lord, who is my Savior, my Redeemer, my Comforter, my Helper, my Healer, my Provider, and my Friend.

The Jewish Maid: Force for Healing

Most Christians do not realize that under the new covenant of Grace we have untold blessings. We have infinitely more blessing than the Israelites were promised under the old covenant. Listen to the words of the blessings of obedience given to the Old Testament saints:

> Then it shall come to pass, because you listen to these judgments, and keep and do them, that the LORD your God will keep with you the covenant and the mercy which He swore to your fathers. And He will love you and bless you and multiply you; He will also bless the fruit of your womb and the fruit of your land, your grain and your new wine and your oil, the increase of your cattle and the offspring of your flock, in the land of which He swore to your fathers to give you. You shall be blessed above all peoples; there shall not be a male or female barren among you or among your livestock. And the LORD will take away from you all sickness, and will afflict you with none of the terrible diseases of Egypt which you have known, but will lay them on all those who hate you. (Deuteronomy 7:12–15)

True to His covenant promise, during the years that God's people wandered in the wilderness, no one's garments wore out, no one's sandals broke down, nor did their feet swell. Their tents didn't wear thin or decay, and no one got sick and died. They were fed manna from the sky and quail on the ground. Their God fought for them and vanquished all their enemies. He provided gushing rivers of water from a rock, and He turned bitter water sweet. Under the new covenant of His pure, unadulterated grace, God supernaturally sustains and restores all that we have by His resurrection life and power, which means we will see abundantly more of His blessings than those who lived under the old covenant (Deut. 8:4).

While the Israelites wandered in the wilderness, there was none feeble among the tribes (Ps.105:37). Part of God's new covenant blessings is our healing. It is not His desire that any one of us be sick or suffer diseases, aches and pains. Jesus's entire ministry was marked by one healing miracle after another. No one who came to Him went away empty-handed. Only a fraction of His miracles were actually recorded; in reality, there were so many more. As His shekinah-queen-priestesses, we were designed to be a force for healing on our planet. Maybe we don't have the gifts of healing *yet*, but each one of us can minister healing through our words, wisdom, counsel, song, teaching, prophesying, worship, comfort, service, and help. We are the Lord's comforters and helpers, His ministering angels of healing in this broken, fallen world. He gave each of us His authority and power, His very glory, and each one of us makes a difference in our sphere of influence.

Second Kings records many of the prophet Elisha's miracles. One story is about Naaman, a commander of the Syrian army, who was a mighty man of valor and a great and honorable man in the eyes of his king, but he was also a leper. On one of his army's raids, he brought back a captive, a young girl from the land of Israel. She waited on Naaman's wife. The Jewish maid said to her mistress, "If only my master were with the prophet who is in Samaria! For he would heal him of his leprosy" (2 Kings 5:3). Naaman's wife shared with her husband what her Jewish maid had reported. Naaman then relayed her word of testimony to his master, the king. With haste, the king of Syria wrote a letter of introduction for Naaman to hand to the king of Israel and then encouraged Naaman to leave for Israel immediately.

Naaman took ten talents of silver, six thousand shekels of gold, and ten changes of clothing. As soon as he arrived, he gave the letter to the king of Israel, which explained that Naaman was there to be healed of his leprosy. The king discussed with Elisha what the commander required, and then He directed Naaman to go to Elisha's house. Elisha sent a message with Gehazi, his servant, to go and meet the commander, telling him to go and dip in the Jordan River seven times and he would be healed. Naaman was furious that the man of God did not come personally and make a big production over his healing. He complained that all the waters in his country were better than any of the waters of Israel. He asked, "Could I not wash in them and be clean?" (2 Kings 5:12) So in a rage, he turned and headed for home.

His servants pleaded and reasoned with Naaman, saying, "My father, if the prophet had told you to do something great, would you not have done it? How much more then when he says to you, 'Wash, and be clean'?" (2 Kings 5:13) So Naaman went down and dipped seven times in the Jordan, according to the man of God's directions, and as he came up out of the water, his flesh was restored like that of a child. He was clean! Naaman returned to the man of God and said, "Indeed, now I know that there is no God in all the earth, except in Israel; now therefore, please take a gift from your servant" (2 Kings 5:15). Elisha would not take payment for God's healing, so Naaman started for home.

Gehazi ran after the commander, lied in Elisha's name, and asked for two talents of silver and two changes of clothes. When Gehazi returned, Elisha asked him where he had gone. Again he lied and said that he hadn't gone anywhere. Elisha asked him, "Are we now going to get rich off God's miracles?" Therefore, because Gehazi was greedy, Elisha told him the leprosy of Naaman will now cling to you and your descendants forever. Gehazi left Elisha's presence, leprous and as white as snow.

God says in Exodus 15:26, "I am the Lord that heals you." Psalm 107:20 tells us, "He sent His word, healed them, and delivered them from their destruction." When a leper approached Jesus for healing, he was doubtful whether Jesus would be willing to heal him. "Jesus put out His hand and touched him, saying 'I am willing; be cleansed.' Immediately his leprosy was cleansed" (Matt. 8:3).

When a woman who had suffered with a bleeding issue for twelve years approached Jesus, she came from behind Him and touched the hem of His garment. Instantly, she was healed. Like the leper, she took a great risk to approach Jesus in public because both of them were considered unclean and could have been stoned for coming out amongst the crowds with their afflictions. Both demonstrated great faith. Jesus felt power go out of Him, and He asked, "Who touched me?" (Luke 8:45) When the woman could see He knew it was her, she came trembling and fell down before Him, declaring before everyone that she was healed. Jesus's response to her was, "Daughter, be of good cheer, your faith has made you well. Go in peace" (Luke 8:48).

The gospels are filled with stories of Jesus healing, casting out demons, raising people from the dead, feeding the hungry, and ministering in every way imaginable. Everyone who came to Him with a problem left satisfied. Nothing was too hard for Him. Matthew tells us, "They brought to Him all who were demon-possessed. And He cast out spirits with a word, and healed all who were sick, that it might be fulfilled which was spoken by Isaiah the prophet, saying: 'He Himself took our infirmities and bore our sicknesses'" (Matt. 8:16–17). Isaiah tells us that Jesus has borne our sicknesses and griefs and He has carried our pains and sorrows and has given us physical healing. The chastisement for our peace was laid upon His back and Isaiah declares that by His stripes we are healed (Isa. 53:4–5).

Jesus was beaten and whipped to an unrecognizable, bloody pulp, His visage more marred than any man, so that He could purchase our healing once and for all. With every lash from the cat-o'-nine-tails, with every piece of His flesh that was torn off His body, He delivered us from every sickness, every disease, and from every ache and pain. We have been completely redeemed from every shred of the curse. Jesus became our curse and paid the ultimate price for our curse by allowing Himself to be scourged nigh unto death. He purchased our right to every manner of healing so that we may say with confidence, "By His stripes I am healed!"

Naaman's Jewish maid is a type of Holy Spirit because she directed Naaman to healing. She informs, she reasons, and she gives hope. Romans 5:5 tells us, "Now hope does not disappoint, because the love of God has been poured out in our hearts by the Holy Spirit who was given to us." Our part is to not give up. Jesus is our beginning and our end. He has the final word, not our sickness or disease. Psalm 103:3 declares that He heals all our diseases. Psalm 147:3 assures us that He heals the brokenhearted and binds up their wounds. In Philippians 2:10, it states that your problems must bow to Jesus's name. Jesus already paid the price for heart disease, cancer, diabetes, arthritis, and every other disease. In the name of Jesus, they must bow to His power and authority and submit to what He has already accomplished on the cross for us.

Like the Jewish maid, we are His powerful shekinahs, and we are a force for healing on our planet. Jesus is our manna from heaven, our bread of life, and He gives us His supernatural power to feed, nourish, and heal those in our sphere of influence. John 6:57 tell us that "those who feed on Me will live because of Me!" So call it forth! (Rom. 4:17) As His queen-priestesses our words carry power (Rev. 1:6, Eccles. 8:4) and if a priestess pronounces someone clean, healed, or blessed, then it is settled (Deut. 21:5). Pray for healing hands. Ask God to manifest His Glory through you.

Start with yourself and your family. God has healed me of a knee injury, back injury, and I am presently praying for healing in a thumb joint. While I was in Sicily, I contracted a severe bout of food poisoning. The pain was excruciating and enough to double me over. My twin sister laid hands on me, prayed for my healing, and instantly the stomach pains were gone. When we do not experience instantaneous healing, we mustn't feel discouraged. Sometimes, healing is immediate, like my stomach pains, but more often than not, healing happens by degrees. When we are praying for a condition and we see a twenty percent improvement, then it should restore our faith and revive our Spirit to receive the next eighty percent.

When Jacob heard that his son Joseph was alive and that he was the governor over all the land of Egypt, his heart fainted within him, because he did not believe it. He thought the news was impossible until he saw the ten wagons loaded with all the good things of Egypt that Joseph had sent home with his brothers. The Bible says that when Jacob "saw the wagons of Egypt…, the spirit of Jacob their father revived" (Gen. 45:27). When we see the miracle manifestations of God's healing or provision, it revives our spirit and gives us the faith to believe for more.

Jesus says to each of us, "Rise up, O you glorious shekinahs, and walk in the fullness of your healing." He tells us, "Do not look at the things which are seen, but at the things which are not seen. For the things which are seen are temporary, but the things which are not seen are eternal" (2 Cor. 4:18). We should see ourselves healed. Do not focus on your condition, but see yourself divinely restored in Jesus's name. His Word says, "All the promises of God are 'Yes' and 'Amen' in Him" (2 Cor. 1:20). Bible hope sees all God's promises and His eternal provisions as truth, and it sees all the temporal things that contradict God's word as temporary and changing.

God is not a liar. He assures us that "I am the Lord who heals you" and "By His stripes we are healed" (Exod. 15:26, Isa. 53:5). Jesus asks us, "Who has believed our report? And to whom is the arm of the Lord revealed?" (Isa. 53:1) "Arm" in this verse means power, strength, might, force, and help. As His precious shekinahs, I hope we can all respond, "I believe your report, Lord, every word, and I thank You that You have revealed to me that all Your power, Your strength, and Your help is mine. I receive Your miracle manifestation of healing, and I declare that every sickness, disease, ache, and pain must bow to the precious name of Jesus. You are my Jehovah Rapha, and I proclaim myself and my loved ones healed!"

Revelation

Once I believed Jesus's miracle manifestations were for another people from another time, but now I know that Jesus is the same yesterday, today, and forever.

Prayer of Praise

Thank You, Lord, that You have sent Your Word and healed me. You have delivered me completely from disease, destruction, and death (Ps. 107:20). Your Word declares, "By Your stripes I am healed and by Your blood I am blessed" (Isa. 53:5). When You speak of my healing, You always speak in the past tense (Ps. 103). Your healing is already mine; riches and honor are in my left hand, and length of days is in my right hand. No one who came to You for healing left empty handed. All who came to You received what they came for, and that includes me. Lord, I claim in Your precious name and by the resurrection life and power of Your blood complete and utter healing over every part of my body. I claim every condition divinely healed and that every affliction must flee in Your great and mighty presence. I pronounce every miracle manifestation of healing is mine today and forever. Thank You, Jesus, for Your miracle healing in my body.

Sarah Blessing: Renewal of Health, Youth, and Beauty

Have you ever beheld the face of a father who is completely besotted over his precious daughter? Immediately, I think of my employer, and of how he looks at his little girl, how his face literally radiates every ounce of love and adoration that he has for his little princess. Or I think of how much Rhett Butler adored and doted on his sweet little Bonnie in the movie *Gone with the Wind*. While many women have not experienced that kind of love from their fathers, hopefully we can all see in our mind's eye what rapt adoration looks like, whether we have seen it for ourselves or have merely observed it in the movies or have seen it exquisitely described in a good book. If we can visualize that look of adoration and devotion, multiply it by infinity, then we begin to get a glimpse of just how lovingly our Heavenly Father looks at us.

In 1 Peter 3:6 God calls us daughters of Sarah. Why Sarah? There are lots of notable women in the Bible, so why are we called the daughters of Sarah? Sarah means princess. He is telling us that we are his precious heavenly princesses. We are told in Genesis that Sarah was very beautiful, so beautiful in fact that twice heathen kings took her into their harems. God is telling us that in His eyes we are gloriously beautiful. The most remarkable thing about Sarah, though, is that God blessed her with renewal of her health, youth, and beauty. God reversed all the ravages of the curse in her body to the extent that she conceived and bore a son at ninety-five. Believe it or not, she was sixty-five and ninety when she was pursued by two different kings for her outstanding beauty. Part of God's pure, unadulterated grace is that He supernaturally renews and restores our bodies, as well as preserves all that we have.

The Israelites were under His pure grace when they left Egypt. No one got sick, no one died, and nothing that they owned wore out (Neh. 9:21). It was only after ten of the twelve leaders, who were asked to go and spy out the Promised Land, came back with a negative, faithless report that God lifted His grace over the nation of Israel. Only two men, Joshua and Caleb, gave a faithful account. They saw that the land was everything God had promised and more, they believed God had already given it to them, and all they had to do was to go in and possess it. Joshua and Caleb understood God's heart and intentions, and because of their faith, God allowed His grace to remain on them. Neither Joshua nor Caleb aged during the forty years that God had the Israelites wandering around in the wilderness. The unbelieving part of the tribes got sick and died, but Joshua and Caleb were as strong at eighty-five as they were at forty. When it came time to conquer the Promised Land, Joshua and Caleb fought with the same strength and vigor as those who were a generation younger than themselves (Josh. 14:10–12). God's grace includes supernatural renewal and restoration of our bodies.

Part of the blessings of the grace covenant that God cut with Abraham is the renewal of our health, youth, and beauty. Abraham was a hundred years old when he conceived Isaac (Gen. 21:5). At ninety-five, God would have had to reverse Sarah's menopause. God assures us and demonstrates to us through the story of Abraham and Sarah, that nothing with Him is impossible. In Second Peter, we are exhorted to believe that those who have obtained the precious righteousness of faith through Christ already possess the following blessing:

> Grace and peace be multiplied to you in the knowledge of God and of Jesus our Lord, as His divine power has given to us all things that pertain

to life and godliness, through the knowledge of Him who called us by glory and virtue, by which have been given to us exceedingly great and precious promises, that through these you may be partakers of the divine nature, having escaped the corruption that is in the world through lust. (2 Peter 1:2–4)

As His heavenly princesses, His grace is multiplied to us. Through His Shekinah glory and godly virtue, He has given us His divine power over every aspect of our lives, making us partakers of His divine nature. At the cross, when He returned to us His glory, He gave us dominion over the lusts of the flesh, over the corruption that is in the world, over the entire perversion of Satan's realm. His grace allowed Sarah to escape the corruption of the flesh so she could embrace His great and precious promises. If you remember, Sarah laughed when the Lord told her that she was to deliver a son at ninety-five. She thought it completely ridiculous that someone her age could bear a child. Yet, when God makes a promise, nothing is too preposterous for Him.

The apostle Paul encourages us not to lose heart when various trials and tribulations stand in the way of our dreams and desires. What God says, He will do. Paul tells us:

For this reason I bow my knees to the Father of our Lord Jesus Christ, from whom the whole family in heaven and earth is named, that He would grant you, according to the riches of His glory, to be strengthened with might through His Spirit in the inner man, that Christ may dwell in your hearts through faith; that you, being rooted and grounded in love, may be able to comprehend with all the saints what is the width and length and depth and height—to know

the love of Christ which passes knowledge; that
you may be filled with all the fullness of God.
(Ephesians 3:14–19)

When we know all that is ours in Christ Jesus, when we are
rooted and grounded in the knowledge of the immeasurable breadth
of His love for us, then, like Sarah, we may be filled with all the fullness of God, meaning every blessing He intended us to have.

The Spirit, our Shekinah Glory, bears witness with our spirit
that we are the children of God, and if children, then heirs—heirs
of God and joint heirs with Christ (Rom. 8:16–17). And as Jesus is
right now, exalted and lifted up, divinely whole, forever young, so
are we in this world (1 John 4:17). We are of God, and we have overcome the corruption of the world because greater is He that is in us
than he that is in the world (1 John 4:4). God the Father raised Jesus
from the dead and seated Him at His right hand in heavenly places
"far above all principality and power and might and dominion, and
every name that is named" (Eph. 1:21). This means that when we
are in Jesus, then we are above every last shred of the curse, including
premature aging.

In the Bible, God says He has given us 120 years to live
(Gen. 6:3). Why then is our life span so short? How many of us even
know that God has given us 120 years? I did not know this until
only a couple of years ago. So many of us, believe God is angry and
disgusted with us, and we buy into every negative report the devil
brings our way. We do not recognize that we have bought into a lie.
We are not aware, that if we are saved, then we are under God's pure,
unadulterated grace and favor. Suffering under the condemnation
and judgment of the law shortens lives. If we believe that we are a
disappointment to God, we will be constantly stressed and full of
worry, anxiety, fears, guilt, and shame. This kind of stress shortens
lives and kills people. Satan is so gleeful when he has us under this
level of deception, because he is the one who is hell-bent to steal, kill,
and destroy us. He is the one who hammers us with health problems,

strife within relationships, untoward disasters, and all the negative circumstances that wreak chaos in our lives.

The tragic thing, is that we give him permission to do this to us when we refuse the gift of the cross and, instead, cling to the law. Job is a great example of this. He said, "The thing I greatly feared has come upon me and what I dreaded has happened me" (Job 3:25). Job spent a lot of energy fretting, worrying, and fearing for his children. He was continually offering sacrifices on their behalf before the Lord. Instead of placing his faith in God's goodness and protection, Job worried and fretted. Therefore, when Satan wants to sift us like wheat, he uses the very things that we have already given him dominion over.

If we believe that God is against us, that He is going to punish us for every wrongdoing that we deserve, then we give Satan permission to come against us with sicknesses, diseases, accidents, and every imaginable negative circumstance which comes straight from the pit of hell. But when we know who we are in Christ, and we know all that is ours because of the finished work of the cross, then we know we are covered by His divine favor and protection. We can come boldly before His throne of grace, and we can be confident that it is God's heart to richly bless us, and His greatest pleasure to prosper and protect us.

Our part in receiving God's blessings under the new covenant is to *hear Him* (Luke 9:35), then *believe Him* (Acts 16:31), *speak His word and promises* (Rom. 10:6), and *ask* (James 4:2). When Jesus was transfigured, the Shekinah glory came down and surrounded Him in a cloud, and a voice came out of the cloud, saying, "This is My beloved Son. Hear Him!" (Luke 9:35) What God is emphatically saying is, "Hear the Words of My Son, Jesus! Hear His words of forgiveness, mercy, and grace! Hear all that He has accomplished for you! Hear His words of no condemnation! Hear His words of blessing! Hear and believe Him! Then speak His Word, His promises, and His faith pictures! The righteousness of faith speaks, so speak His righteousness, power, glory, and authority over your lives!

Lastly, ask!" We have not, because we ask not! Even more importantly, because we serve a great and mighty God, ask *big*! Believe Him for every promise, believe Him for net-breaking, boat-sinking provision and prosperity, and believe Him for the renewal of your health, youth, and beauty.

Jesus came that we may have life, and that we may have it more abundantly (John 10:10). Believe that with every breath we take, God gives life to everything that is dead in us (that is our Sarah blessing), and He calls those things that don't yet exist, as though they did (Rom. 4:17). Which things don't yet exist? Every healing, every renewal, every restoration, every promise, and every provision—in other words, every blessing and every anointing that God says is already ours. God says that happy is the person who finds wisdom and who gains understanding. Length of days is in her right hand (our Sarah blessing), and in her left hand riches and honor (our Abraham blessing) (Prov. 3:16). Believe that God is opening to you all His good storehouses of treasure (Deut. 28:12) and blessing you with every possible blessing (Gen. 12:2).

We are living in the times of restoration (Acts 3:19-21). Jesus's death and resurrection has restored to mankind His glory. He has restored our soul, our identity of who we are in Christ (Ps. 23:3). He has restored our position and made us blood-bought heirs of our Most High God (Rom. 4:13). He has restored our provision, raises everything that is dead in us to resurrected life and power, and calls every blessing spoken over us into existence (Rom. 4:17). He restores our possessions, everything that is already ours in Christ Jesus (Obad. 1:17). He restores our health and heals all our wounds (Jer. 30:17). He restores our beauty and keeps us forever vibrant and radiant (1 Pet. 3:6). He restores our youth, keeping us strong, dynamic, and energetic (Ps. 103:5). He restores our place (Deut. 6:10). He restores our prosperity (Gal. 3:13). And He restores our years and redeems wasted opportunities (Joel 2:25). He is a restorer of life and a nourisher of our old age (Ruth 4:15). The apostle Paul tells us that when Jesus presents His glorious church to His Father, we will not have spot or wrinkle or any such thing, but we will be holy and without blemish (Eph. 5:27). We need to see ourselves as Jesus sees us—without spot or wrinkle, without a single blemish—only radiant, glorious, and holy in His sight!

In 1 Peter 2:9, God says, "But you are a chosen generation, a royal priesthood, a holy nation, His own special people, that you may proclaim the praise of Him who called you out of darkness into His marvelous light." In Revelation 1:6, Jesus tells us, "To Him who loved us and washed us from our sins in His own blood, and has made us kings and priests to His God and Father; to Him be glory and dominion forever and ever: Amen." If we belong to Jesus, He calls us queens and priestesses. Ecclesiastes 8:4 proclaims, "Where the word of a king is, there is power," and Leviticus 27:12 states that whatever "the priest shall set a value for it, whether it be good or bad; as you, the priest, value it, so it shall be." God calls us His queen-priestesses, and He tells us, where the word of a queen is, there is power, and whatever His priestesses place value on, He values. God is telling us that we get a double portion of speaking power; he gives us power as queens and as priestesses "by their word every controversy and every assault shall be settled" (Deut. 21:5). He gives us His authority as His queen-priestesses.

He has given us His glory and dominion over the kingdom of darkness forever and ever. Isaiah 55:11 also tells us that our words shall not come back void. He says, "So shall My word be that goes forth from My mouth; it shall not return to Me void, but it shall accomplish what I please, and it shall prosper in the thing for which I sent it." As His royal priestesses, our words carry power—what we declare blessed is blessed; what we pronounce healed is healed, and what we demand restored is restored. In whatever way we assess our lives divinely blessed, they will be blessed!

Once, not so very long ago, I saw myself as disgusting and wretched in His sight, but now, thanks to His glorious grace and the truth of His word, I know that I am His heavenly princess, His royal priestess, and His most beloved daughter. Like Sarah, He showers on me the renewal of my health, youth, and beauty. With every breath I take, I am being translated into my glorified image. Every day, I speak into existence my Sarah blessing over my body. I pray, "But we all with unveiled face, beholding as in a mirror the glory of the Lord, are being transformed into the same image from glory to glory, just as by the Spirit of the Lord" (2 Cor. 3:18) The Bible tells us the more that I look to Jesus and behold His beautiful face, the more I worship and adore His glorious presence, the more I am being transformed into His image, which is forever young, perfectly healthy, and divinely radiant. I love Psalm 103! It reveals so much about God's heart toward us:

> Bless the Lord, O my soul, and all that is within me, bless His Holy Name!
> Bless the Lord, O my soul, and forget not all His benefits:
> Who forgives all your iniquities? Who heals all your diseases?
> Who redeems your life from destruction?
> Who crowns you with lovingkindness and tender mercies?
> Who satisfies your mouth with good things, so that your youth is renewed like the eagles?
> Bless the Lord, you His angels, who excel in strength, who do His word.
> Bless the Lord, all you His hosts, you ministers of His, who do His pleasure.
> Bless the Lord, all His works, in all places of His dominion.
> Bless the Lord, O my soul! (Ps. 103:1-5; 20-22)

How many sins does God forgive? How many diseases does He heal? All of them, right? He tells us that He satisfies our mouth with good things. This means he delights in giving us our necessities as well as our heart's desires at whatever age or situation we may be in. We wear His crown of glory; therefore, His lovingkindness and tender mercies chase after us and aggressively hunt us down. He likens the renewal of our youth to an eagle, because eagles are strong, overcoming, soaring, and victorious. In this passage, angels heed the voice of His word. Now who gives voice to His word? We do! Every time we speak His word, the angels must heed our voice. What else do the angels do? They do His word! As we speak God's promises and words, hosts of angels spring into action to accomplish all that He says. After spending three weeks in fasting and prayer, the angel Gabriel came to Daniel and said, "I have come because of your words" (Dan. 10:12).

What is God's pleasure that all the hosts of heaven are ministering? In Psalm 35:27, we are told, "Let the Lord be magnified, Who has pleasure in the prosperity of His servant." It should gladden our hearts to know that God has ministering angels assigned to work on our provision, protection, and prosperity. He also assures us, the works of His ministering angels is blessed in all places of His dominion. All the hosts of heaven are working on our behalf and must respond to the voice of God's word. That is why the righteousness of faith must speak, because we are the ones who command and activate our ministering angels to work on our behalf. Hence, we should cry out with a loud voice, "Bless the Lord, O my soul, and all that is within me, bless His Holy Name! Bless the Lord, O my soul, and forget not all his benefits, bless His Holy Name!"

We are God's glorious shekinahs, His heavenly princesses, His royal priestesses, and His most beloved beautiful daughters. He has given us the most precious gift of the renewal and restoration of our physical bodies. We are called the daughters of Sarah because God esteems us as His beloved princesses, and He blesses us with the renewal and restoration of our health, youth, and beauty. His heart is to unleash upon each one of His princesses His pure, unadulterated grace just as He blessed Sarah. I would encourage His precious daughters to begin praying for God to release upon us the fullest measure of our Sarah blessing, so that each one of us may begin to walk in the fullness of all that is ours in Christ Jesus and begin experiencing the miracle manifestations that are already ours as His heavenly princesses.

Moses Anointing: Radiant Countenance

When Moses went up to Mt. Sinai the second time to meet with the Lord, he asked if he could see God's glory. God responded that He would allow Moses to see all His goodness as He passed by, but that no man could see God's face and live. So God tucked Moses into a cleft of a rock, He put His hand over it, and then He allowed Moses to see only His back as His Shekinah glory passed by. From this exposure to God's Shekinah, Moses's face took on a permanent radiance of God's glory. The Bible also tells us that when Moses would enter the tabernacle, the pillar of cloud descended and stood at the door of the tabernacle, and the Lord talked with Moses as a man speaks to his friend (Exod. 33:9–11). Exodus continues to tell us, "Now it was so, when Moses came down from Mount Sinai (and the two tablets of the Testimony were in Moses's hand when he came down from the mountain) that Moses did not know that the skin of his face shone,... and they were afraid to come near him" (Exod. 34:29–30). In order to minister to the people, Moses had to cover his face with a veil so as not to frighten them.

Under the old covenant, God's Shekinah glory would only temporarily rest on a person. Under the new covenant, His glory indwells us. That is why we have all seen some Christians who literally radiate His glory. Their countenance shines with His presence. Haven't we all met Christians who we knew were saved just by looking at their faces? We can see the Holy Spirit shining in them. This should be how the world sees every one of His glorious shekinahs. Every one of us should radiate His lightest brightest shimmering glory. Seriously, if our Comforter/Helper has taken up residence in our being, it should be evident to all.

When I was a broken, frail, fractured Christian, so full of wrong beliefs, although I was saved, and I had His glory within me, my light was buried under a shroud of wrong thinking. My light was smothered by the heavy darkness of lies from the enemy. We cannot shine when we are under the ministry of death. We can only shine when we are confident that we are loved and adored by God despite our mistakes and failures. We can only radiate His love and glory when we know with certainty that His everlasting love and boundless glory is ours no matter what. Jesus told us:

> You are the light of the world. A city that is set on a hill cannot be hidden. Nor do they light a lamp and put it under a basket, but on a lampstand, and it gives light to all who are in the house. Let your light so shine before men, that they may see your good works and glorify your Father in heaven. (Matthew 5:14–16)

When God made man, He crowned him with glory and honor. His glory clothed man like a garment. Adam's whole being was gloriously radiant. Jesus said, "And the glory which You gave Me, I have given them [us], that they may be one, just as We are one" (John 17:22). Jesus returned to us the glory that Adam was originally blessed with, but forfeited when he sinned. Today, instead of wearing His glory like a garment, it indwells us and fills up our entire being, saturating us from the inside out. Our bodies radiate His glory from within, and our shekinah pours out of our countenance as light. Our eyes are truly the windows to our soul. His glory can be seen pouring out from our eyes and radiating from us. Given we wear clothes over our physical bodies, like Moses, it is our faces that reveal His glory. Jesus wants each one of His precious shekinahs to be a living testimony of His Grace, and to let His glory shine before men. Thanks to Christ's finished work on the cross, we are crowned with His glory and honor. So arise, and let your light so shine that the world may see the radiance of His glory and grace that dwells within you.

Revelation

Once I saw myself as disgusting and wretched in His sight, but now I know I am His heavenly princess, His royal priestess, and His most beloved daughter.

Prayer of Praise

Thank You, Jesus, for revealing to me my true identity in You and for restoring my soul. Thank You for elevating me to the position of blood-bought heir to Your heavenly throne. You call me a daughter of Sarah because I am Your princess, as well as Your royal priestess. You also call me a comforter and a helper, the same word You use for the Holy Spirit. Not only am I called to be a comforter and a helper, I am a covering and a minister of Your radiance as Your precious shekinah. Thank you, Jesus, for exalting me to Your heavenly position, and for making a place for me next to Your right hand, from whence comes all my help. You infuse me with Your resurrection life and power from the atomic level outward, so that there isn't even an electron's bit of space left for any part of the curse. Every shred of the curse has to flee in Your Great and Mighty Presence. Hence, why I am utterly and completely healed, renewed, and restored by Your Sarah blessing upon my body. Thank You, Jesus, that I am the apple of Your eye and that Your every thought toward me is only precious. My heart swells with joy and gladness because of who I am in You.

Abraham Blessing: Releasing Financial Provision and Prosperity

If we want to see a picture of what pure grace looks like, then we should look at how God relates with Abraham. Abraham lived long before the law was given, so He had no concept of God as a harsh taskmaster. On the contrary, Abraham loved God and believed in Him; therefore, God considered Abraham righteous because of his faith. Abraham was living in the city of Haran at the northwestern tip of the Tigris-Euphrates river valley, when God told Abram to go to the land of Canaan. The Lord said to Abram:

> Get out of your country, from your family and from your father's house, to a land that I will show you. I will make you a great nation; I will bless you and make your name great; and you shall be a blessing. I will bless those who bless you, and I will curse him who curses you; and in you all the families of the earth shall be blessed. (Genesis 12:1–3)

The Lord blessed Abram and made him very rich in livestock, silver, and gold. God prospered everything Abram set his hand to. Even though Abraham appeared to be rather cowardly at times, as in trying to pass off his beautiful wife as his sister when heathen kings wanted her for their harems, yet God always rescued Abraham and continued to mightily bless him. Or perhaps, acquiescing to these foreign kings was an act of great faith, because to deny them Sarah may have cost both of them their heads; therefore, Abraham and Sarah may have had no choice but to rely on God to supernaturally rescue them from the tyrannical lust of these heathen kings. Whatever the real scenario, God miraculously intervened on both accounts and rescued Sarah.

The covenant that God cut with Abraham wasn't based on Abraham's obedience; it was solely based on God's grace. God imputed righteousness to Abraham based on Abraham's faith, not his works. So even if Abraham was more concerned with saving his own skin than protecting the welfare and reputation of his wife, God did not think less of Abraham because of his human frailty and failures. There was no expectation from God for perfect behavior from Abram, because He only saw him through His lens of grace. Since the law had not yet been given, there were no rules to measure one's self against, either. Blessedly, Abraham did not have to worry and fret over whether his behavior was good enough to earn God's favor, because he had absolutely no concept or framework for what that would look like. Their relationship was gloriously uncomplicated. Abraham believed God, and God blessed him.

After Abram had settled in the land of Canaan, the word of the Lord came to Abram in a vision saying, "Do not be afraid, Abram. I am your shield, your exceedingly great reward" (Gen. 15: 1). Abram was concerned that he did not yet have an heir, and the Lord reassured him that his descendants would be more than the stars in the heavens. Abram believed the Lord, and God accounted it to him for righteousness. Abraham asked God, "Lord God, how shall I know that I will inherit it?" (Gen. 15:8) God asked Abram to bring him a three-year-old heifer, a three-year-old female goat, a three-year-old ram, a turtledove, and a young pigeon. Then Abram brought all these to the Lord, cut them in two down the middle and placed the pieces opposite each other. God caused a deep sleep to fall over Abram, and then a smoking oven and a burning torch, His Shekinah glory, and God the Father passed between the two pieces coming from opposite directions. Typically, Abraham would have been required to pass between the sawn pieces to make a covenant binding, but instead, the glory of the Lord passed by the pieces on Abraham's behalf to make the covenant with God the Father.

In essence, God is saying, "I am swearing by myself and establishing a covenant with you based on My goodness and My promises. It is not based on what you do." In other words, Abraham can't do anything to muck it up, because the covenant was between God the Father and His Shekinah glory. The implication for cutting a covenant, is that if one of the people breaks the promise they have made, then may it be to them as the sawn pieces of the animals. Why this covenant is pure grace, is because Abraham has no responsibility in keeping the promise nor can he do anything to cause it to fail. It is a gift, and he only benefits. The Lord promises to give Abraham and His descendants the Holy Land, to bless him mightily, to make him a blessing to others, to make his name great, to make him a mighty nation, and to give him innumerable descendants—and all that is required of Abraham is to believe God. The Lord also gave Abram a new name, *Abraham*, which means "father of a multitude."

This Abrahamic covenant is a picture of the new covenant, but this time, God the Father cuts the covenant with God the Son on our behalf. What is so amazing is that the Lord tells us in Romans, "For the promise that he would be heir of the world was not to Abraham or to his seed through the law, but through the righteousness of faith" (Rom. 4:13). In Galatians we are told, "If you are Christ's, then you are Abraham's seed, and heirs according to the promise" (Gal. 3:29). What promise are we heirs to? Through our righteousness of faith in Christ, we are heirs of the world—heirs to every good and perfect gift that our Heavenly Father delights to lavish on His Son. This includes the whole circle of earthly goods, endowments, riches, pleasures, and advantages.[1]

---

[1] Joseph H. Thayer, *Thayer's Greek-English Lexicon of the New Testament* (Peabody, MA: Hendrickson Publishers Marketing, LLC, 2015), 357.

God's said, "I will bless you and make your name great, and I will make you a blessing" (Gen. 12:2). We are heirs to every possible tangible and spiritual blessing that the earth has to offer, as well as everything contained in the storehouses of heaven. God also promises that we will be a blessing. We cannot be a blessing unless we have been blessed. God blessed Abraham with exceedingly great wealth and rewards, and in like manner, He wants to bless us so we can be a blessing to our families, our churches, and those around us.

God tells us in Psalms, "My covenant I will not break, nor alter the word that has gone out of my lips" (Ps. 89:34). God cut a new covenant with us using the blood of His own precious Son, and we should not waver in our belief that what God says, He will do. He assures us, "Blessed be the Lord, who daily loads us with benefits, the God of your salvation" (Ps. 68:19). He tells us, "The blessings of the Lord makes one rich, and He adds no sorrow with it" (Prov. 10:22). Jesus tells us, "But seek first the kingdom of God and His righteousness, and all these things will be added to you" (Matt. 6:33). Psalms tells us, "My heart shall rejoice in Your salvation. I will sing unto the Lord, because He has dealt bountifully with me" (Ps. 13:5–6). God's heart is to give us a superabundant supply. In Philippians, He said, "My God shall supply all your needs according to His riches in glory" (Phil. 4:19). The covenant that God cut with Abraham is a faith picture of the covenant He has cut with us. God the Father cut the new covenant with God the Son, and we can't do anything to muck it up. That is why it is a gospel of Grace. Like the Abrahamic covenant, it is so simple—we believe in God's Son, and God blesses us.

Even more amazing is the fact that every blessing is already ours, as heirs to His throne of grace. In Joshua, the Lord says, "I have given you a land for which you did not labor, and cities which you did not build, and you dwell in them; you eat of the vineyards and olive groves which you did not plant" (Josh. 24:13). God speaks in the past tense. He has already dealt bountifully with us. Like Abraham, we should believe that God is more eager to bless us than we want to be blessed, that it is His heart and greatest pleasure to prosper us

(Ps. 35:27). This kind of faith imputes to us His righteousness, and blessings are on the head of the righteous (Prov. 10:6). Faith is the substance of things hoped for, the evidence of things not seen (Heb. 11:1). Faith believes what God says, whether we see it yet or not. "The Spirit bears witness with our spirit that we are the children of God, and if children, then heirs—heirs of God, and joint heirs with Christ" (Rom. 8:16–17), and Jesus has blessed us with every spiritual blessing in heavenly places in Christ (Eph. 1:3). Every blessing is already ours.

Once, not so very long ago, I believed I was overlooked and unworthy to receive God's blessings, but now I know that I am the righteousness of my God in Christ, the seed of Abraham through faith, and an heir according to the promise. As an heir of the world through the finished work of Christ, I know I have a blood-bought right to a life full of meaning and purpose. I have a blood-bought right to walk in divine renewal of my health, youth, and beauty. I have a blood-bought right to prosperity and exceedingly great abundance. I have a blood-bought right to preferential treatment, because I am deeply loved, highly favored, and greatly blessed. I have a blood-bought right to grow in His wisdom, knowledge, truth, power, joy, peace, and rest. I have a blood-bought right to be a blessing to others. I have a blood-bought right to prosper, even when the economy is bad, and I have a blood-bought right to the fullest measure of my Abraham blessing and my Sarah blessing. Amen, I receive my inheritance as a beloved daughter of the Most High!

Joseph Anointing: Blessed to be a Blessing

So many faith pictures reveal God's heart to bless those who are under His pure, unadulterated grace. When we look at the story of Joseph, we see God's hand of grace over every aspect of his life. No matter how many times Satan came against Joseph with ill circumstances and false accusation, God was with Joseph. While Joseph was standing naked on an auction block to be sold into slavery, God called Joseph a successful man. Everyone around Joseph could see that the Lord prospered everything he put his hand to. Satan threw at Joseph incredibly discouraging circumstances, but true to God's word, He orchestrated every bit of it for good to exalt Joseph and place him in a position of influence so he could ultimately save his entire family from poverty and starvation.

Joseph's character was remarkable because he never harbored bitterness. He was betrayed by his brothers, sold into slavery, falsely accused by Potiphar's wife, and thrown into a dungeon. At every turn, he continued to trust that God was with him and that He would handle it. God would not let anything keep Joseph down. In due time, God exalted him from the pit to the palace, made him the head, not the tail, and made him a lender, not a borrower. God brought Joseph riches second only to Pharaoh. It is God who gives us the power to get wealth, the kind of wealth that prospers us and doesn't corrupt. Like Joseph, when we put our trust in God as our Provider, He will exalt us in due time.

Our part in receiving our Joseph anointing is to give the Lord something to bless. God said He blessed all the works of Joseph's hand. Joseph was moving forward, working, producing, creating, learning, trying new things, and using His God-given wisdom and talents right where he was at. God wants us to step out in faith, to contribute in our areas of gifting, and to pursue our dreams. He puts in our hearts those secret desires to pursue and do, and He wants us to believe that with Him all things are possible. He wants each of us to rise to our full potential. We should never say, "Never" or "I can't!" Move forward in faith, knowing that with God we can do whatever we put our minds to. Like Joseph, hold fast to God's pronouncement of blessings on your life:

> Blessed shall you be in the city, and blessed shall
> you be in the country. Blessed shall be the fruit
> of your body, the produce of your ground and

increase of your herds, the increase of your cattle and the offspring of your flocks. Blessed shall be your basket and your kneading bowl. Blessed shall you be when you come in, and blessed shall you be when you go out. The Lord will cause your enemies who rise against you to be defeated before your face; they shall come out against you one way and flee before you seven ways. The Lord will command the blessing on you in your storehouses and in all to which you set your hand, and He will bless you in the land which the Lord your God is giving you. (Deuteronomy 28:3–8)

God is saying to you, "Believe that My favor and grace surrounds you like a shield, that it goes before you, it hovers over you, and it follows after you. Believe that My goodness, mercy, and blessings hunt you down. Every time you speak My blessings over your life, I call forth legions of angels to attend to My word. I love you with the same ferocity that I loved Joseph and I gave you these stories to encourage you in your faith. Through these faith pictures, I am saying, 'This is Who I Am.' It is My heart to bless you, and it is my greatest pleasure to prosper you. I am showing you that all you have to do is reach out and seize what is already yours as heirs to My throne of grace. My Son suffered grievously to make you joint heirs with Himself and to give you all His riches in glory. So don't be shy. Ask big, believe big, and expect big, for I am your great and mighty God who blesses you *big*!"

Benjamin Generation Blessing: Five Times the Grace

God revealed to Joseph Prince that we are living during a very special time. During the final generation before Christ returns, there is going to be an unprecedented outpouring of grace upon God's people. We are seeing it as we speak—a grace revolution is sweeping the planet. God has unleashed His grace message to believers as never before, and it is spreading like wildfire across the globe. It is a most exciting time to be a Christian. The veil of the law is being lifted from the eyes of God's people and they are walking into the marvelous freedom of His glorious grace Life. Jesus's gift of the gospel of unmerited and unearned favor and blessing is being taught and propounded, and believers are apprehending the fullest measure of all that they are and all that they have in Christ Jesus.

As Pastor Prince was studying the life of Benjamin, Jacob's youngest son and Joseph's younger brother, he noticed that the number 5, the number for grace, was stamped all over Benjamin's life. In the pastor's book *The Benjamin Generation*, he presents all the details of this fascinating faith picture. When Joseph was reunited with his brothers, he blessed them with food and a change of clothing, but to Benjamin, his full-blooded brother, he showered him with five times more food and clothing than he gave to his ten half-brothers, as well as gifted Benjamin with three hundred pieces of silver. "Three hundred" means "God appears," and silver stands for "redemption."

God is saying that He will appear to youngest son, who represents the last generation before Christ returns, and He will redeem them mightily, blessing them with five times the grace. Like Benjamin, we are the full blood-bought heirs, because the promise that he would be the heir of the world was not to Abraham or to his seed through the law, but through the righteousness of faith in Christ. God tells us, "All these blessing shall come upon you and overtake you" (Deut. 28:2). In other words, you cannot outrun or escape these blessings; they will hunt you down and follow you all the days of your life (Ps. 23:6). As part of the Benjamin generation, we can expect five times the blessings of the generations that have gone before us. We can expect five times the financial provision and five times the renewal of our health, youth, and beauty.

Dektos Blessing: The Acceptable Year of the Lord

Jesus went to Nazareth, where he had been brought up, and as was His custom, He went into the synagogue on the Sabbath and He stood up to read. He was handed the scroll of the Prophet Isaiah. He opened it and began to read,

> The Spirit of the Lord is upon Me, because He has anointed Me to preach the gospel to the poor; He has sent Me to heal the brokenhearted, to proclaim liberty to the captives and recovery of sight to the blind, to set at liberty those who are oppressed; to proclaim the acceptable year of the Lord. (Luke 4:18–19, Isaiah 61:1–2)

When He was done reading, He closed the book and He said to them, "Today this Scripture is fulfilled in your hearing" (Luke 4:21).

According to Thayer, the Greek word for "acceptable year of the Lord," *dektos*, "denotes that most blessed time when salvation and the free favors of God profusely abound."[1] Jesus states this time is here, it is now. He tells us that we can expect God to bless us profusely and superabundantly because this most blessed time is here. Thanks to Christ's finished work on the cross, He won for us a blood-bought right to prosper in every area of our lives. He has given us His power and authority to minister to the poor, to heal the brokenhearted, to open the eyes of the blind, to set captives free, and to proclaim that today, right now, is "the acceptable year of the Lord," the most blessed time when God's unbridled favor and blessings gloriously abound.

---

[1] Thayer, *Thayer's Greek-English Lexicon*, 128.

Spiritual Blessings: Pneumatikos Blessings

In Ephesians 1:3, Paul tells us, "Blessed be the God and Father of our Lord Jesus Christ, who has blessed us with every spiritual blessing in the heavenly places in Christ." The word *spiritual* in Greek is *pneumatikos,* and it means ethereal (not of earth, but heavenly), spiritual, supernatural, and regenerate. It always connotes the idea of invisibility and of power.[1] It pertains to things that belong to the Divine Spirit and references to things that emanate from Her, or exhibiting its effects, and so Her character.[2] This word does not occur in the Old Testament or in the Gospels, but is an after-Pentecost word. We are told that we are blessed with *every* spiritual blessing. This reiterates the truth of the new covenant, that God desires to bless us with every blessing that He delights to shower on Jesus. This means that every blessing characteristic of God and the Holy Spirit is ours.

Since Jesus was God made flesh indwelt by the Holy Spirit, we see that pneumatikos blessings surrounded His ministry. When He needed money, He called it forth from a fish. When the crowds were hungry, He fed them with five small fish and a couple loaves of bread with twelve basketfuls of leftovers. When people came to Him sick, He healed them. When people came to Him with unclean spirits, He chased them out. When loved ones died, He raised them from the dead. These are spiritual blessings because they can only emanate from God. Every spiritual blessing that surrounded Jesus and His ministry surrounds us today. As Jesus is right now, exalted and lifted up, so are we. These are the spiritual blessings we should be praying for and the kind of divine power we should see emanating from the Holy Spirit who indwells us. We can have every expectation of every good and perfect gift from our Heavenly Father because every spiritual blessing is ours.

---

[1] James Strong, *The New Strong's Expanded Exhaustive Concordance of the Bible* (Nashville, TN: Thomas Nelson Publishers, 2010), 205.
[2] Thayer, *Thayer's Greek-English Lexicon,* 523.

High Priest: Order of Melchizedek

In Hebrews, we are told, "For when God made a promise to Abraham, because He could swear by no one greater, He swore by Himself, saying, 'Surely blessing I will bless you, and multiplying I will multiply you.' And so, after he had patiently endured, he obtained the promise" (Heb. 6:13–14). The Bible says,

> When God wanted to guarantee his promise, he gave his word, a rock-solid guarantee—God can't break his word. And because his word cannot change, the promise is likewise unchangeable. We who have run for our very lives to God have every reason to grab the promised hope with both hands and never let go. It's an unbreakable spiritual lifeline, reaching past all appearances right to the very presence of God where Jesus, running on ahead of us, has taken up his permanent post as high priest for us, in the order of Melchizedek. (Hebrews 6:18–20, MSG).

Melchizedek was king of Salem and priest of the Most High God. *Melchizedek* means "king of righteousness," and *Salem* means "peace," so he is also "king of peace." Jesus is called our High Priest forever, according to the order of Melchizedek, because Jesus forever represents us before God. As our representative, Jesus's righteousness becomes our righteousness forever in the eyes of God. As our High Priest, we have an everlasting righteousness because it is forever based on what Jesus accomplished on the cross for us, not on our works. That is why we can boldly say, "I am the righteousness of God in Christ!" (2 Cor. 5:21) Proverb 10:6 says, "Blessings are on the head of the righteous," which means we are continually blessed. The priesthood of Jesus, according to the order of Melchizedek, can only bless as well. Unlike the Levitical priesthood, which blesses as well as curses, Jesus's priesthood only blesses. In other words, we cannot help but be blessed. Proverbs 10:22 tells us, "The blessings of the Lord makes one rich." We can confidently declare we are rich in His mercy, rich in His grace, rich in His healing, rich in His glory, rich in His presence, and rich in His power.

We are forever rich in His superabundant supply! We can boldly declare that it His heart to richly bless us, and His greatest pleasure to divinely prosper us! Every believer has a High Priest who touches our lives with His eternal righteousness, His supernatural divine healing, and every possible dektos, pneumatikos, and Benjamin generation blessing. In other words, we have God's word on it; we are infinitely and gloriously blessed beyond what we could ever think or ask, because we have a High Priest, the Son of Righteousness and King of kings, who stands in our place before God. As heirs to His throne of grace, God now lavishes on us all the love, adoration, and blessing that He lavishes on Jesus. Because our Heavenly Father only sees us through His precious Son, our perfectly righteous High Priest, He proclaims us forever and always His beloved who are eternally blessed!

Revelation

Once I believed I was overlooked and unworthy, but now I know that I am the seed of Abraham through faith, an heir according to the promise, and as a blood-bought heir I inherit all the blessings of Abraham, all the blessings of Sarah, which means God will supernaturally renew, restore, protect, and provide for me all my days.

Prayer of Praise

Thank You, Jesus, for blessing me beyond what I could think or ask. I know that it is Your heart to bless me and Your greatest pleasure to prosper me. Every good and perfect gift that my Heavenly Father desires to lavish on You, He now lavishes on me. I am heir to every earthly and heavenly blessing this world has to offer. The entire circle of worldly and heavenly endowments and blessings are mine because of my Abraham blessing upon my life. I cannot help but be superabundantly and gloriously blessed. Thank You, Lord, that I live in the most blessed time, when the salvation and free favors of God profusely abound. I live in a blessed time of favor, when Your Grace is unleashed in unprecedented proportions. Like Benjamin, I can expect five times more wisdom, knowledge, glory, provision, protection, favor, health, healing, and blessing than any generation that has lived before me.

Thank You, that You make all grace abound toward me, that You have given me an abundance for every good work (2 Cor. 9:8). Thank You, Heavenly Father, for adopting me as Your beloved daughter and for showering on me every possible blessing that Jesus gets and deserves. Your goodness and graciousness toward me literally hunt me down. Thank you, Lord, for Your blessed inescapable covenant of Grace over my life. My spirit is continually revived and renewed with awe and gratitude because I know net-breaking, boat-sinking provision and prosperity is on its way because of who I am in You.

Joseph: Unshakeable Faith and Immeasurable Grace

In Proverbs 31:10, the Bible asks the question, "Who can find a virtuous wife?" I can think of many virtuous wives that I know. A more challenging question for me would be, "Who can find a virtuous husband?" I would have a little harder time answering that question. Matter of fact, there is only one man mentioned in the Bible who was truly virtuous. Joseph, Jacob's elder son, through his beloved wife Rachel, demonstrated admirable character under various trials and temptations.

While Joseph was adored and spoiled by his father, he was hated by his ten half-brothers because he was so obviously favored. Joseph further fueled his brothers' hatred by sharing a dream, one that implied that his brothers would one day bow down to him. His brothers found Joseph so insufferable that one day when they were far from home, they conspired to sell him as a slave to a passing Ishmaelite caravan that was going down to Egypt. When they got home, they told their father that Joseph had been torn to pieces by a wild animal. The Midianites sold Joseph to Potiphar, an officer of Pharaoh and captain of the guard.

The Lord was with Joseph and He called him a successful man. Potiphar saw that the Lord prospered everything that Joseph did; therefore, Joseph found favor in his master's sight, serving him faithfully. In no time, Potiphar made Joseph the overseer of his house; he put all that he had under Joseph's authority, and the Lord greatly blessed the Egyptian's house and fields because of Joseph. Whatever Joseph set his hands to divinely prospered.

Joseph was not only successful in every endeavor, he was also very handsome. It wasn't long before Potiphar's wife noticed how attractive Joseph was and started to flirt with him. She brazenly asked him to lie with her. Joseph refused her and tried to reason with her, but she would have none of it. He told her:

> Look, my master does not know what is with me in the house, and he has committed all that he has to my hand. There is no one greater in this house than I, nor has he kept back anything from me but you, because you are his wife. How then can I do this great wickedness, and sin against God? (Genesis 39:8–9)

She refused to hear Joseph and kept harping on him. One day when the servants were gone, she grabbed his garment and demanded him to lie with her. He fled, leaving the garment in her hand. When her husband got home, she accused Joseph of trying to rape her.

Potiphar threw Joseph in the king's prison, but the Lord was with Joseph and showed him mercy, granting him favor in the sight of the prison keeper. The keeper of the prison put everything in Joseph's hand, and God caused everything he did to prosper. It came to pass that two of Pharaoh's officers, the chief butler and the chief baker, offended the king and were thrown into prison with Joseph. Each man had a dream on the same night, which greatly disturbed them.

When Joseph came in the morning to see to their needs, he saw that they were both very sad. Joseph asked them both, "What is wrong?" They shared that they had both had a dream, and they did not know what it meant. Joseph replied, "Do not interpretations belong to God? Tell them to me, please" (Gen. 40:8). Both men shared their dreams, and Joseph told them that in three days, the butler would be restored to his position, although on the same day, the baker would be hung. It came to pass on the third day, which was Pharaoh's birthday, exactly as Joseph foretold.

Two years later, Pharaoh had a dream that troubled his spirit. He called in all his magicians and wise men to interpret it for him, but they could not. Then the chief butler spoke up and told Pharaoh about Joseph interpreting his and the chief baker's dreams, that both interpretations came to pass exactly as Joseph said. Pharaoh immediately sent for Joseph. He pronounced, "I have heard it said that you can understand a dream and interpret it." Joseph answered Pharaoh, saying, "It is not in me; God will give Pharaoh an answer of peace" (Gen. 41:16). Pharaoh shared his dream, and Joseph interpreted it.

Joseph told Pharaoh that there would be seven years of great plenty, followed by seven years of severe famine. Joseph then counseled Pharaoh to select a discerning and wise man, who should collect one-fifth of the produce of the land during the seven plentiful years, which will be set back and reserved for the seven lean years. Joseph's advice so impressed Pharaoh and his counselors that he put Joseph in charge over all the land of Egypt, giving him power and authority second only to himself. Under Joseph's wise leadership, Egypt richly prospered during the seven years of famine because all the nations of the Middle East came to Egypt to buy grain.

It was during this famine that Jacob sent his ten sons to Egypt to buy grain, but he did not send his youngest son, Benjamin, who was Jacob's youngest son through Rachel. Joseph instantly recognized his brothers, but they did not recognize him because he was dressed as an Egyptian. Joseph tested his brothers to see if they regretted their actions toward him. He wanted to know if they had dealt harshly with his little brother, Benjamin. He threw them in prison for three days, and he listened to their conversations with one another. Then he loaded their donkeys with enough supplies to temporarily combat the famine in their households, he returned their money to their sacks, he kept Simeon in jail, and he demanded that they return with the youngest brother in order to purchase more grain.

Although Jacob was afraid and inconsolable about sending Benjamin with his ten half-brothers down to Egypt, Rueben swore upon the life of his two sons that he would bring the boy back alive. Judah also promised his father that he would be a surety for Benjamin. When they ran out of grain, there was no choice but to go and purchase more food, because the famine was so severe. Jacob finally relented and let Benjamin go with his brothers, although he sent some of the best fruits of their land as a present for Joseph, as well as double the money, returning the money that Joseph had put back in their sacks.

When Joseph saw Benjamin, he had his steward take his brothers to his house, and he ordered a lunch prepared for them. The brothers thought they were taken to Joseph's house because they were going to be accused of stealing the money that they had found in their sacks. They tried to explain what had happened to Joseph's steward, but the steward replied, "Peace be with you, do not be afraid. Your God and the God of your father has given you treasure in your sacks; I had your money" (Gen. 43:23). Then the steward brought Simeon to them. The steward gave them water, washed their feet, and tended to their donkeys.

When Joseph arrived for lunch, the brothers gave him the presents their father had sent with them. Joseph then inquired about his father and the brothers assured him that Jacob was alive and well. Joseph asked them if this was their younger brother. Joseph said to Benjamin, "God be gracious to you, my son" (Gen. 43:29). Then Joseph left the room and wept. He washed his faced and returned to his brothers and ordered lunch to be served. It was against the law for an Egyptian to eat with Hebrews, so Joseph dined apart from his brothers. He sat them according to their birth order, which greatly astonished his brothers. Joseph took the servings to his brothers, but to Benjamin he gave five times as much as the others.

He ordered his steward to fill the men's sack with as much food as they could carry, to return their money to their sacks, and to put Joseph's silver cup in Benjamin's sack. When morning dawned, the brothers were released so they set off toward home. When they had not gone far from the city, Joseph sent his steward to catch up with them and to demand of them, "Why have you repaid evil for good? Why have you taken my master's cup?" The brothers denied stealing from Joseph, and they proclaimed, "With whomever of your servants it is found, let him die, and we also will be my lord's slaves" (Gen. 44:9). The steward responded, "Let it be according to your own words." The steward searched all the sacks from the oldest to the youngest, and as the steward already knew, the cup was found in Benjamin's sack. The whole entourage was taken back to Joseph's house.

As Joseph approached his brothers, he asked, "What deed have you done?" Judah responded, "What shall we say to my lord, how shall we clear ourselves?" Joseph replied, "Leave the one who stole the cup with me to be my slave, and the rest of you can go in peace to your father." Then Judah asked to speak and pleaded, "I beg for the life of my youngest brother for his father's sake. The loss of the boy would bring down our father's gray head with sorrow to his grave, because the life of our father is wrapped up in the life of the boy. We cannot go back without the lad, or it is the same as killing our father. Please allow me to remain as your servant instead of Benjamin." When Joseph saw his brothers' contrition and willingness to protect Benjamin, he broke down and cried. He chased out of the room all his servants, and then he revealed himself to his brothers, saying, "I am Joseph, does my father still live?" (Gen. 45:3) His brothers could not answer him, for they were afraid and greatly dismayed.

Joseph said to his brothers, "Please come near to me." So they gathered round him, and he said,

> I am Joseph your brother, whom you sold into Egypt. But now, do not therefore be grieved or angry with yourselves because you sold me here; for God sent me before you to preserve life. For these two years the famine has been in the land,

and there are still five years in which there will be neither plowing nor harvesting. And God sent me before you to preserve a posterity for you in the earth, and to save your lives by a great deliverance. So now it was not you who sent me here, but God; and He has made me a father to Pharaoh, and lord of all his house, and a ruler throughout all the land of Egypt. (Genesis 45: 4-8)

He instructed his brothers to hurry back to his father and to tell him that his son Joseph was lord of all Egypt. He would give them the land of Goshen, and he would provide for them. Joseph sent carts which could be used to bring his family from Canaan back down to Egypt. He gave each of his brothers a change of clothes, but to Benjamin he gave five sets of garments. And for his father, Joseph sent ten male donkeys loaded with the good things of Egypt and ten female donkeys loaded with grain, bread, and food for his father's journey.

When the brothers reached home and told Jacob that Joseph was alive and was the governor over all the land of Egypt, his heart fainted within him because he didn't believe them. But when he saw all the carts and donkeys loaded with all the good things of Egypt, his spirit revived. With joy he said, "It is enough. Joseph my son is still alive. I will go and see him before I die" (Gen. 45:28). So the Israelites journeyed back to Egypt to the land of Goshen. Then God spoke to Israel in the visions of the night and said,

"Jacob, Jacob!" And Jacob said, "Here I am." God continued, "I am God, the God of your father; do not fear to go down to Egypt, for I will make of you a great nation there. I will go down with you to Egypt, and I will also surely bring you up again; and Joseph will put his hand on your eyes." (Genesis 46:2–4)

Jacob lived in the land of Goshen seventeen years before he passed away. He gave a final blessing on his sons, and when he died, they took his body back to Canaan to bury. Joseph lived 110 years, and he was buried in Egypt. Years later, Moses carried his bones back to Canaan (Exod. 13:19).

Joseph is remarkable for his unshakeable faith in God's immeasurable grace. No matter how negatively circumstances stacked up against Joseph, he never wavered in his faith in the goodness of God. As a young man, Joseph experienced the betrayal of his brothers. Most of us have experienced some form of betrayal, whether from relationships, physical/emotional/sexual abuse, divorce, or even death. Some people can become derailed for years, even for a lifetime, over a betrayal. What is so impressive about Joseph is that he did not allow himself to become bitter. He believed God was bigger than his circumstance, that God would take what man meant for evil against him and turn it to good. That is amazing faith! I have wasted years being bitter, rather than trusting God with my hurts. The story of Joseph inspires me to never again travel down that road, but to immediately take my hurts to God, and trust that He will make it right.

Again, when Potiphar's wife was hounding Joseph to sleep with her, Joseph did not cave on his principles. How many men exhibit this kind of virtue? A beautiful woman was throwing herself at Joseph, and his first response was to consider all that God had done for him and determine that he would not possibly sin like that against his God. Joseph was more worried about what God would think, than what man thinks. He put honor for His God before the needs of his flesh and bodily comfort. Again, Potiphar's wife lied and betrayed Joseph's virtue, and his reward was to get thrown in prison. Wouldn't that cause most people to become bitter—to be falsely accused, to know you are innocent, to know that you were doing everything you were supposed to be doing, you were behaving honorably, but *still*, you get thrown into prison? Most people would shake their fist at God and scream, "Why me, Lord?" Most of us would be raging within and consoling ourselves by plotting vengeance of some kind.

I remember one time my husband, son, and I took on a roofing project that one of our friends didn't have time for. It was a twelve-by-twelve pitch, metal roof on a log house in North Pole, Alaska. We got paid half up front, which paid for the new metal, but when the job was done, the guy stiffed us for the second half, our labor. It was the worst roof we ever did. Every night after coming off the job, my leg muscles quivered near to collapse after climbing up and down a forty-five-degree pitch all day. Every single sheet metal screw was a bugger to seat because it takes so much force to pierce metal. It was such a difficult job, and then the guy cheated us our labor. I was so furious I wanted to kill him. I plotted all manner of evil things I could do to him. In the end, I had to let it go because we were a small mom and pop, and we didn't have the energy or desire to endure a lengthy court battle. A lawyer would cost more than the job, which is exactly what the thief counted on.

Unlike Joseph, it took me quite a while to forgive that man. In the moment, the last thing I was thinking about is how God will make this thing right. Back then, I did not understand God's grace, so it was not easy for me to offer grace. Now that I am older, and I understand that it is God's heart to bless me, I believe I could respond more graciously under a similar circumstance. Why Joseph is so remarkable is that he was just a young man when he was sold into slavery. He was so young to have such unshakeable faith. Most young men that age are quick to fight and quick to rage. Joseph, on the other hand, just set about to do the best he could right where he was at. He was a servant in Potiphar's household, so he sought to be the best servant he could be. Because he committed to God everything that he did, God caused all the works of his hands to prosper. It was so obvious that in a relatively short period of time, Potiphar entrusted the running of his entire house and fields into Joseph's hands.

When he got thrown into the king's prison, he set out to be of service to the prison keeper, and the keeper could see immediately that everything Joseph managed prospered. The keeper of the jail turned everything over to Joseph's care. It is awe-inspiring to see that kind of faith. Joseph just put one foot in front of the other, looked for ways to serve and just did it, and he trusted God to work out all the other details of his life. I am sure he clung to his vision that God was going to exalt him for a purpose, yet in the meantime, he persevered doing the best he could do and trusted God to fulfill his promises in due time. He believed God had a purpose for his life, and he knew nothing man could do could stop the plans God had for him. Slave blocks and prisons were temporary setbacks, but with God, setbacks do not set Him back—His plans for us will prevail.

When Joseph was brought before Pharaoh to interpret his dream, he didn't just share the meaning of the dream; he used his gifts and particular talent for management to lay out a plan to prepare the country for the years of famine to come. Pharaoh was so impressed with his quick mind for management strategies that he made Joseph the overseer of all the lands of Egypt. Joseph was not reticent when his moment came to shine before Pharaoh. He stated the problem, he came up with a solution, and God is the one who exalted him. Like Joseph, if we move forward exercising our gifts, strengths, and talents, we can trust God to put us in the right place at the right time.

While Joseph was standing on the slave block, God called him a successful person. It does not matter where we are standing in relation to our vision. We may be on the bottom-most rung of the ladder, but steadfast faith declares, "With God, I am a successful person, and I can do all things through Christ who strengthens me!" Our part is to continue putting one foot in front of the other, moving forward toward our goal, and trust that God will exalt us in due time. Our part under the new covenant is to trust that God is bigger than our circumstance. Our circumstances do not have the final word—God does. God declares us blessed and successful and faith believes what God says about us. God is telling us to think like Joseph. Get a vision for who you are in Christ and for all that is yours as blood-bought heirs of the Most High, and then don't compromise your vision. Set your eyes upon Jesus, and then climb up your ladder one rung at a time.

Speak out loud your vision throughout the course of your day. Boldly declare, "I am an outrageous success! I am deeply loved, highly favored, and greatly blessed! Thank you, Jesus, that, like what you did for Joseph, You are blessing all the works of my hands, and You are making all my gifts precious stones that prosper me. Thank you, Lord, that You are making my gifts diamonds, rubies, sapphires, emeralds, opals, and pearls in my hands, that You are making everything I touch to prosper."

The righteousness of faith speaks! Our words have creative power. Think successful, act successful, and speak successful. You may be starting at ground zero, but take heart, for God has already declared you a successful person. Like Joseph, place your unshakeable faith in His immeasurable Grace, then watch God unleash His pure, unadulterated grace, His manifest glory, and His miracle-sized blessings in every area of your life.

Revelation

Once I felt such a failure, but now I know I am an outrageous success, that He blesses all the works of my hands and He makes all my gifts precious stones that prosper me.

Prayer of Praise

Thank you, Jesus, that You see me as a success. Like Joseph, You cause me to triumph no matter what obstacles the enemy has strewn across my path. You cause my mountains to melt like wax in the presence of the Lord, and nothing is too hard for You, nor can anything or anyone prevent the plans you have for my life. Lord, it may look bad, feel bad, and even be bad, but with You on my side, I have Your promise that it will not stay bad. You assure me that You take whatever man or Satan means for evil against me, and You turn it into my good.

I do not need to feel frustrated when obstacles arise, because I know that You are bigger than any obstacle, and Your plans for me will prevail. Thank You, Jesus, that You have my back. Thank You that You bless all the works of my hands, and You make all my gifts precious stones that prosper me. Thank You that You are exalting me from the pit to the palace, from pauper to princess, from the tail to the head, from a borrower to a lender, and from last to first in a position of influence. It gives me the greatest comfort to know that You are for me, Lord, and because You are aggressively and persistently for me, who can stand against me? Thank You, Jesus, that in Your eyes and in Your perfect plan, I am a success.

The Prodigal: Living Intimately and Infinitely Loved

The most precious faith picture that shares the depth of our Heavenly Father's love for us is found in Luke 15:11–31, in the parable of the lost son. In this story, Jesus is sharing a picture of His Father, who is also our Father. Parables are stories that contain a deeper meaning. Jesus used simple stories to share spiritual truths. He created faith pictures to paint heavenly truths on the canvas of the common person's understanding, using ordinary events to share extraordinary truths. Faith pictures bring glimpses of spiritual enlightenment into our temporal understanding. Jesus wanted us to understand our Heavenly Father's intimate and infinite love for us, so He gave us the story of the prodigal son.

Jesus told the story of a man who had two sons. The younger son said to his father, "Give to me my inheritance now. I don't want to be here anymore. I want to get as far away from here as possible." With a saddened heart, the father gave to his youngest his portion of the inheritance and watched as his son walked away. Multiple times a day, the father would scan the horizon, watching and waiting, hoping his son would return.

The son journeyed to a far country and spent his entire inheritance on partying, drinking, and loose women. As long as he had money, he had lots of friends, but as soon as his money was gone, wasted on prodigal living, the boy was left all alone. A severe famine arose in the land where he was living, and the boy started to go hungry. Eventually, he scrounged a job feeding pigs, and he was so hungry he resorted to eating the slop thrown to the pigs. In desperation, he thought, "My father's hired servants live better than this. They get three square meals a day and a decent place to sleep. I could go back to my father and ask him to hire me as a servant, and then, I won't starve."

As the boy was walking home, he memorized a speech he would say to his father. He would say, "Father, I have sinned against heaven and before you, and I am no longer worthy to be called your son. Make me like one of your hired servants" (Luke 15:18-19). When he was almost home, his father saw him from way off, and instantly, great love and compassion welled up in his heart for his son. The father lifted his robes and ran as fast as he could to greet him, falling on his son's neck, and kissing him. The son started to recite the speech he had memorized, but his father cut him off and hollered at his servants to bring out the best robe, to put a ring on his son's finger, and to bring the best sandals for his son's feet. The father ordered his servants to kill a fatted calf so they could all eat and be merry, for he declared, "For this my son was dead and is alive again; he was lost and is found" (Luke 15:24). Then everyone joined in the party of celebration for the prodigal son.

When the older brother came in from the fields and heard music and dancing, he called one of his father's servants to ask him what all the commotion was about. The servant informed him that his brother had returned, so your father has killed the fatted calf in his honor, and we are all celebrating. The oldest brother was furious and would not go in. His father came outside and pleaded with his eldest to come join the celebration. The eldest replied,

> Lo, these many years I have been serving you;
> I never transgressed your commandment at any
> time; and yet you never gave me a young goat,
> that I might make merry with my friends. But as
> soon as this son of yours came, who has devoured

your livelihood with harlots, you killed the fatted
calf for him. (Luke 15:29–30)

The father answered his son, saying, "Son, you are always with me, and all that I have is yours. It was right we should make merry and be glad, for your brother was dead and is alive again, and was lost and is found" (Luke 15:31–32).

Jesus hid several profound truths in this story. In the natural, we all empathize with the eldest son, but in the spiritual, most of us are like the youngest. At some point in our lives, we, knowingly or unknowingly, have turned our backs on God. Some of us may have never heard of Jesus; therefore, we are ignorant of His gift of grace. While some of us have heard the gospel message, we may have chosen to walk away from it. All of us at some point in our lives were dead to salvation and lost in our sins, like the youngest son.

God is revealing to us in this story that he is always waiting and always looking for his lost ones to turn and walk back to Him. When He sees one of His own make that turn toward Him, He lifts up His robes, and He runs to embrace His precious sons and daughters in Christ. God is never in a hurry, nor does He need to rush, but Jesus is telling us that God is relentlessly pining and yearning for His children to be saved, and if we take that first step and invite Jesus into our hearts, like a flash, our Heavenly Father will be there with all the hosts of heaven who will be leaping and dancing and rejoicing and singing, "Glory! Hallelujah! My child was once lost but now is saved!"

The eldest son is a picture of me for forty years of my Christian experience. I served God to the best of my ability and tried my best to follow all His commandments, but I did not know God or understand His heart. I viewed God as a harsh taskmaster who was just waiting to smack me flat the minute I stepped out of line. Since I knew I was an overall failure at keeping all His commandments, I felt I deserved whatever torment He was going to dish out. Like the eldest, I would never have dreamed to ask God for anything special because I knew I didn't deserve it and, therefore, God would only say no, so why even ask?

The eldest son is a picture of the mind-set of a person under law, not Grace. They do not understand God's heart of love toward His beloved sons and daughters, but instead, they see God the Father as stingy and hard-hearted. Jesus is telling us, all that God has is already ours. The eldest could have asked for the fatted calf at any time, and the Father's heart would have rejoiced to give it to him. God delights when we ask of Him, and it genuinely blesses His heart to give us the desires of our hearts. When we delight in Jesus, God delights in blessing us, and He wants us to ask.

Sometimes, like the eldest son, we see the "law-keepers" ridicule or despise the "grace children" because law-keepers place a high value on "their works," while the children of grace place high value on Jesus and "His finished work" on the cross. Law-keepers are sure that it cannot be that simple, that obedience is more important than faith, that works carries more weight than forgiveness. Law is black-and-white and dependable, while grace is utterly gray and unfair. Law-keepers are the first to point out who is not worthy of grace, although seldom do they complain when grace is offered to them. The eldest was furious that his father forgave his younger brother, but he would have willingly received his father's forgiveness should he have made a mistake.

We all understand that in the natural, the youngest did not deserve his father's forgiveness, but Jesus is telling us that in the natural, none of us deserve forgiveness. We all fall short and have sin in our lives. Jesus is saying sinners, just like the prodigal son, don't deserve forgiveness, neither can we earn it—forgiveness is a gift from God. This gift cost God dearly; it cost Him His dear Son. Jesus suffered terribly in order to give us His gift of unearned, undeserved, unmerited forgiveness, favor, and grace. Like the prodigal, he didn't earn it or deserve it, but it was a gift freely given by his father. We are like the prodigal. It does not matter what our past is or what we have done, God says, "Shhh, I remember those things no more! I rejoice because once you were lost, but now you are found!"

God lifts up his robe, and He runs toward us. He wraps us in His loving arms, and He hugs and kisses on us. He wraps us in Jesus's robe of righteousness, so that when He looks at us He only sees Jesus in all his holiness, perfection, and glory. He puts on our finger a ring of authority, giving us all the power and dominion that belongs to Jesus. He puts His best sandals on our feet so that we are shod with the preparation of the gospel of peace. He surrounds us with His presence, protecting us at every turn. He prepares a feast for us, lavishing on us every good and perfect gift that He lavishes on Jesus. He fills our hearts with gladness and joy, infusing our lives with His pure, unadulterated grace, His Shekinah glory, His great and mighty presence, and His wondrous-working power. He tells us, "As Jesus is, right now, exalted and lifted up and seated at the right hand of our Heavenly Father, so are we!"

If we take the love that we have for our children, and we multiply it by infinity, then we begin to get a glimpse of just how much our Heavenly Father loves us. If we, being imperfect parents, know how to give good gifts to our children, how much more will our Heavenly Father give good things to those who ask Him? Jesus is telling us in the story of the prodigal that our Father's love for us is immeasurably intense and immense. He knows everything we have ever done, and He loves us anyways. That is because His love is not based on our obedience, what we have or haven't done; it is only based on Jesus, on His obedience and what He has done for us. Praise God, our salvation does not depend on us, but on One who is an absolute surety! Like the prodigal, we rejoice that once we were lost in sin and without hope, but now we know we are forgiven and that God loves us intimately and infinitely beyond anything we could possibly imagine! Such is the Father's heart for His beloved!

Revelation

Once I believed God forgave other people's sins, but mine were too offensive, but now I know that thinking was blindness and pride, that Jesus was beat to a bloody, unrecognizable pulp to pay for MY sins, therefore, I am completely and utterly forgiven.

Prayer of Praise

Thank You, Jesus, for Your unfathomable love for me. No one is outside the reach of Your mercy or beyond the realms of Your forgiveness, including me. I have a Savior who knows me intimately and yet still loves me. He numbers the very hairs on my head. I love my own children with every fiber of my being, yet I have never counted the number of hairs on their heads. If I take how much I love my children, my husband, my animals, and I multiply that by infinity, then I only begin to get a glimpse of how great is my Heavenly Father's love for me. Thank You, Jesus, that You will never give up on me, nor will You ever forsake me. It gives me immense confidence to know that my Heavenly Father's love for me is intimate and infinite. You are the very best Father God I could possibly imagine. The depth of Your care, concern, kindness, and tender mercy toward me is incomprehensible and unknowable. Bless You, sweet Heavenly Father, for Your magnanimous, matchless, immeasurable love for me.

The BIG Lie: Expounded and Exposed

As God declared in Genesis, we have an enemy to our souls—Satan. He is the prince of this world, and the author of all enmity, warring, and strife on our planet. His strategy has been the same since time immemorial; he is the father of lies who seeks to steal, kill, and destroy us. The *big lie* he uses again and again, to great success I may add, is the belief that "my tribe is better than your tribe" or "my religion is superior to your religion" or "my politics are more rational than your politics" or "my sex is dominant and superior over your sex." The underlying premise is always the same; it is the belief that "I am in some way superior to you." It is the age-old Big Lie that man uses to justify domination, subjugation, genocide, racism, sexism, torture, and all manner of abuse. The belief that "I am superior to you, therefore, you do not deserve respect or the basic human rights that I am entitled to or [in the extreme case] even the right to live" is rooted in the disgusting cesspool of rottenness, evil, lies, and murder that permeates Satan's ugly realm.

Satan's strategy to cause strife, warring, and enmity in the world never changes. It was the same lie that allowed white men to justify in their own minds their right to keep black slaves. In their perverted thinking, they subjugated black people into a nonhuman category. Today, we look back and say, "How sick was that!" It was evil to the point of preposterous, but millions of people bought into the big lie. The same lie allowed the Germans to consider the Jews as a people less than human to justify their annihilation of six million human beings. Mostly, one could not even physically distinguish a Jew from a German, but hundreds of thousands of Germans bought into the Big Lie that they were the superior race which they thought perversely justified exterminating their neighbors, friends, and even family members. Today, we look back and say, "That was incredibly vile and seriously messed up! How could such a heinous atrocity like that happen?"

It happens because once Satan has his vicious talons sunk deep into a person and he swallows the Big Lie hook, line, and sinker, then the depths of cruelty that man is capable of knows no bounds. Under the spell of the Big Lie, we see the powers of darkness, depravity, wickedness, and hell uncovered and unleashed in its most malicious fury.

We see the Big Lie manifested all over the world in the way men treat women. In many cultures, still today, women are treated as pieces of chattel, as objects to be used for sex, as second-rate citizens, and in some places, as barely even human. In some countries, Satan's war against women is as grossly evident as it is appalling. Across our planet, Satan's rampant war against women and their offspring has never been more evident or apparent than by what can be daily observed in the global sex trade.

Even in this country, some men view women as pieces of meat to be used solely for man's pleasure and are barely afforded a soul. They excuse away all manner of exploitation, abuse, perversion, and disrespect based on the Big Lie that they are superior to women; therefore, in their twisted mind-set, they think women do not deserve to be treated with the same level of consideration, honor, and value that men get and deserve. Under the delusion of the big lie, they think women were created to be controlled, dominated, subdued, and used for pleasure. Man apart from God, especially those under Satan's spell of deceit, can be so bent in their thinking, which only serves to advance Satan's war against women and their children.

Another place we can see the Big Lie at work is in some of our churches. Some men believe that the Bible gives them the right to dominate and subdue women. They believe that women were created to submit to men, that they should be seen, not heard, and just do what they are told. These men will take great offense at the thought that women were represented in the Godhead from the beginning, that the Shekinah glory is feminine, and that the Holy Spirit, our Comforter/Helper, reflects the feminine heart of God. These men view themselves superior to women, and they believe women need to stay in their place: underneath men's feet. Doesn't this sound just like the thinking white men used to subjugate the blacks and keep them in their place? White preachers even used their Bibles to try and justify their mistreatment of the blacks, the same way some preachers will try to perpetuate the age-old lie to justify treating women as Biblical afterthoughts, second-rate citizens, and instruments of servitude.

When God blessed His creation and told Adam to, "Be fruitful and multiply; fill the earth and subdue it; have dominion over the fish of the sea, over the birds of the air, and over every living thing that moves on the earth" (Gen. 1:28), He didn't tell Adam to subdue other humans, or even more specifically, to subdue and subjugate women. He was referring to creatures. At the moment this commandment was given, Eve wasn't even created yet, so obviously she was not grouped into the "things" category that "creep over the earth." In 1 Peter 3:7, the Lord tells husbands, "Husbands, likewise, dwell with them (your wives) with understanding, giving honor to the wife, as to the weaker vessel, and as being heirs together of the grace of life, that your prayers may not be hindered." God's instruction to husbands was to live with their wives in an understanding and compassionate way, giving honor to them as blood-bought heirs to the throne of grace; otherwise, God is not going to hear their prayers.

God did not say, "Husbands, subdue, dominate, and control your wives." On the contrary, He says, "Husbands love your wives, just as Christ loved the church and gave Himself for her" (Eph. 5:25). There is no place in the New Testament that shows Jesus trying to dominate, subdue, or in any way trying to act tyrannical toward His church. We see the opposite in fact; He loved the church so much that He laid down his life for her. So when we see a Christian man with the attitude that women are lesser beings who should keep quiet and just obey, I believe what we are seeing is the same old Big Lie.

In God's eyes, all humans have equal value and standing. No one is more esteemed than anyone else. He loves each one of us with an equal amount of passion and devotion. Men are His mighty "princes" and women His precious "princesses." Marriage is not a master–slave relationship; it's a covenant designed to create completeness. Men bring to the marriage physical strength, godly leadership, provision, and protection; and women bring relational strength, domestic provision, sensitivity, support, comfort, as well as beauty and grace.

The Lord, the husband, and the wife form a perfect trinity. As a couple submits themselves to the Lord and one to the other, we create a three-strand cord that is not easily broken. I submit that true submission to one another works best in a mutual atmosphere of honor, respect, and trust. It also helps if you have confidence that the one you are submitting to loves you and has your best interests at heart. God asks wives to submit to their own husbands as to the Lord and to respect him as the head of the family as Christ is head of the church. According to *Strong's Concordance*, *submit* in the nonmilitary sense means "to have a voluntary attitude of cooperation, assuming responsibility, and helping in carrying a burden." In other words, we should be a *helper* to our husband. As the husband loves, honors, and adores his wife, as Christ loves the church, the wife reveres, honors, defers to, and respects her husband as unto the Lord. This mutual respect and devotion, which has its center in Jesus Christ, epitomizes the unbreakable, everlasting bond of the marriage covenant.

Some Christian husbands confuse the nonmilitary word for *submit* with the military term *subdue*. Again, God commanded men to subdue the creatures of the earth, not his wife, or other people groups. While these same men may feel I am encouraging people to rebel against the church's age-old order of things, my response would be, "That's right!"

Just because we have thought a certain way for thousands of years doesn't make it true. For ages, people thought the world was flat, but it wasn't true. Further exploration revealed that their long-standing belief was incorrect. In the same way, the entrenched ugly mind-set about women in our churches must be exposed for what it is—the Big Lie!

Nowhere in Scripture did Jesus bully, manipulate, dominate, or abuse anyone. The Lord only dealt tenderly and gently with the women and children who surrounded Him. So where does this mind-set come from, that thinks it is okay to dominate, subjugate, and demean women? I submit that I have already answered that in chapter 1. Satan is at war with us, and all the ugly, wrong attitudes that we face are the result of his handiwork.

In no way do I want to cast aspersions on the millions of wonderful godly husbands who love, honor, and cherish their wives just as Christ loves His bride, the church. If we could take a peek into the lives of these men, I know we would see rich, rewarding, blessed marriages and families. God says He hears these men's prayers, and He showers them with His divine favor and blessings. These men understand what it means to live with their wives in an understanding and tender way. Yet, most of us can name several Christian men who treat their wives harshly, rudely, and disrespectfully. It is these men I hope to reach with the truth of women's identity in the eyes of God.

In some of our churches, we see an attitude that women's place is teaching children, babysitting in the nursery, and serving and hosting, but they are not esteemed as copastors, coleaders, and coteachers. They are not exalted as equal partners in the Godhead and have not been allowed to operate in all the spiritual gifts which are unique to their position as comforters/helpers. Hopefully, once our churches see the Big Lie for what it is, we will correct our thinking about women, and we will be able to move forward in right relationship with one another and in ministry. I hope that our pastoral leaders will embrace women's rightful position in the Godhead, that our gifts, talents, and services will begin to be valued and utilized in the ministry, and that we will be honored and esteemed for our strengths as His shekinahs.

Another insidious version of the Big Lie is the personal one, the one we direct at ourselves. It is the accusing voice that convinces us that God is disgusted and angry with us. Hosea 4:6 says, "My people are destroyed for lack of knowledge." The lie I believed—that I was less than pond scum in the eyes of God—destroyed my relationship with Him, and obliterated any joy I might have had in the Lord. No one is drawn to someone whom they believe hates them. We are naturally repelled by critical judgment and condemnation, and we run from it as fast as we can. That is why it is so vital to understand the difference between the old covenant and the new. Many of God's people are defeated by their lack of knowledge of who they are in Christ. I spent forty years living in defeat because of this lie, completely missing the whole point of the cross. Oh, I taught children the grace message, and I even wrote songs about it, but when it came down to believing how much God loved me, I disqualified myself. In the darkness of my deception, I thought the grace passages only applied to children and the "good Christians," not to pathetic failures like me. I was nearly destroyed over my lack of knowledge.

When Satan gets his vicious talons sunk into us, it puts a veil over our hearts and minds, blinding us to all the benefits that are ours, thanks to the finished work of Christ. Yet, when we hear the truth of the gospel, its full message, that we are heirs to everything that Jesus gets and deserves, then His amazing Grace removes the veil and the blinders, making us "undevourable" by the enemy's lies. When we place our trust in Jesus, and look only to the power and authority of the cross, it makes the lies from the pit of no effect.

For forty years, I lived defeated, depressed, and nearly destroyed because I did not know who I was in Christ and all that was mine under His new covenant of grace. Once I was so very blind, but now, glory, hallelujah, I see! Now I know that I am His precious shekinah, His royal priestess, and His most beloved daughter! I sit with Jesus at my Heavenly Father's right hand, exalted and lifted up above every principality and power! I am the apple of His eye, His glorious treasure! Every thought He has toward me is only precious. Listen to the words of Psalm 139: "How precious also are Your thoughts to me, O God! How great is the sum of them! If I should count them, they would be more in number than the sands" (Ps. 139:17–18).

When we know beyond know that our Heavenly Father loves and adores us beyond anything that can be measured, there is no room in our hearts and minds for the Big Lie. We are completely consumed and saturated with the *Big Truth*:

> For I'm persuaded that neither death nor life, nor angels nor principalities nor powers, nor things present nor things to come, nor height nor depth, nor any other created thing, shall be able to separate us from the love of God which is in Christ Jesus our Lord. (Romans 8:38–39)

Jesus wants each one of us to know that we are precious in His sight, that we are the apple of His eye, His glorious treasure. We are nestled under the protective wing of His mighty Cherubim, and nothing and no one can pluck us from our Heavenly Father's hand. He continually showers us with His goodness, mercy, and loving kindness. Every good and perfect gift that God desires to lavish on His Son, He now lavishes on us. His loving righteous endearing thoughts toward us are more in number than the sands of the sea. Our hearts cry out, "O how precious is my blessed Lord because His unsearchable, unfathomable love for us made it possible for us to love Him!"

As we are loved, so ought we to love one another, to esteem others as greater than ourselves. We know or recognize other Christians by the way they love one another. John tells us:

> If someone says, "I love God," and hates his brother; he is a liar; for he who does not love his brother whom he has seen, how can he love God whom he has not seen? And this commandment we have from Him: that he who loves God must love his brother also. (1 John 4:20–21).

Christ died for sinners; the worst of us and the least of us. No matter what our past, our failures, our race, our politics, our religion, or our sex, Christ died for all of us. He looks at each and every person, and He says,

> Precious, O how precious are My thoughts toward you!
> O God, how great is the sum of them!
> If I should count them, they are more in number than the sands of the sea.
> Precious, O how precious are you to Me!

Revelation

Once I believed I was less than nothing in the eyes of God, but now I know that was the Big Lie; I am precious in His sight, and His thoughts toward me are only precious.

Prayer of Praise

Thank You, Lord, that I am the apple of Your eye, Your treasure, and Your precious daughter. Thank You for opening my eyes to the truth of who I am in You. I am exalted to the highest position in the universe, and I am nestled under the mighty wings of Your cherubim. I am infused and saturated with Your divine radiance,

Your great and mighty presence, and Your wonder-working power. Fill me, O Lord, with the truth of Your great love for me and with the truth of all that I can accomplish in You. Make me Your powerhouse of healing, compassion, and grace midst the brokenness of this world. Make Your truth triumphant over me and help me to walk in Your supernatural victory. Make Your Shekinah glory emanate from every pore of my being and allow me to make a difference in the world. Empower me to have an impact for Your glory.

Shekinah: Fearsome in All Her Glory

"Shekinah" is defined as "the Divine Presence, the numinous [spiritual, supernatural] immanence of God in the world…a revelation of the holy in the midst of the profane."[1] According to Jewish tradition, "Shekinah" is light, as in the verse "the earth did shine with His glory" (Ezek. 43:2). John Keyser, from Hope of Israel Ministries, remarks in his article, "YEHOVAH's Shekinah Glory," that rabbis teach

> "This is the face of the Shekhinah" (Avot diRabbi Natan [18b–19a]; see also Chullin [59b–60a]). Both the angels in heaven and the righteous in *olam haba* (the world to come) are sustained by the radiance of the Shekinah (Exodus Rabbah 32:4, B'rakhot 17a).[2] [See Ps. 19:1, Ps. 8.]

When God said, "Let there be light: and there was light" (Gen. 1:3), He was announcing the appearance of His Shekinah glory. Dr. Scofield comments in his reference Bible that this was not a creative act, but that the sense was that it was "made to appear; made visible."[3] The sun, moon, and stars were not created

---

[1] *Encyclopedia Judaica* "Shekinah," 1349–1351.
[2] John D. Keyser, "YEHOVAH's Shekinah Glory," Hope of Israel Ministries, accessed September 16, 2016, http://www.hope-of-israel.org/glory.htm.
[3] C. I. Scofield, "Genesis 1:3," in *The Scofield Reference Bible: The Holy Bible: Containing the Old and New Testaments: Authorized Version* (New York: Oxford

until day four. The light God unveiled was His manifest presence in His Shekinah glory, which sustains the universe and everything in it. Father God, Jesus, and His Holy Spirit have always existed, but in the days after His creation, when God decides to manifest Himself to man, He will do so through His Shekinah glory. When Moses asked to see God, God told Moses, "You cannot see my face; for no man shall see Me, and live" (Exod. 33:20). Therefore, He tucked Moses into a cleft in the rock, He covered Him with His hand, and then He passed by, showing Moses His Shekinah glory (Exod. 33:22).

Keyser quotes an ancient Hebrew scholar:

> According to Saadiah Gaon (882–942 C.E.), the *Shekhinah* is identical with *kevod ha-Shem* (the glory of God), which served as an intermediary between God and man during the prophetic experience. He suggests that the "glory of God" is the Biblical term, and *Shekhinah* the Talmudic term for the created splendor of light which acts as an intermediary between God and Man, and which sometimes takes on human form. Thus when Moses asked to see the glory of God, he was shown the Shekhinah, and when the prophets in their visions saw God in human likeness, what they actually saw was not God Himself, but the Shekhinah [see Ezekiel 1:26; 1 Kings 22:19; & Daniel 7:9].[1]

Since the beginning of the story of man, God has sought to dwell, to *shakan* with man. The meaning of the word Shekinah (the One Who dwells) reminds us that we did not seek to dwell with God, but He sought to dwell with us. God desires an intimate rela-

---

Univ. Press, 1945), 3.
[1] Keyser, "YEHOVAH's Shekinah Glory."

tionship with us. We love Him, because He first loved us (1 John 4:19). The picture of God's Shekinah glory shining on the mercy seat of the ark of the covenant and dwelling between the wings of the cherubim is a beautiful picture of how God's glory shines in the hearts of all those who have asked Jesus to be their Savior, their Mercy Seat, and how She dwells and radiates in the earthly temple of our bodies. Every shred of our sinfulness and rebellion is forever covered by the blood of Jesus, who is our Mercy Seat. Like the two tablets of stone, our sins lay forever hidden under the mercy seat to be remembered no more. Now when God looks at us, all He sees is His glorious radiance shining in us because His Shekinah indwells us. This should fill our hearts with awe and thanksgiving that it is God Who first expressed His desire to dwell with us, and that He loved us so much that He made a way for us to love Him.

From the moment we were created, God's Shekinah hovered, waiting for the Father's instructions to intervene, to guide, and to bless. The Shekinah's first assignment was one of protection. God stationed (shakan) cherubim at the east of the garden of Eden to guard the way to the tree of life, which after the fall, man was no longer allowed to eat. As the story of man progresses, cherubim will be associated with the Shekinah. In Genesis 15:17, 18, in reference to God cutting a covenant with Abraham, it says, "Behold, there appeared a smoking oven and a burning torch that passed between those pieces." In other words, God put Abraham to sleep and then He made a covenant based on Himself by having His Shekinah glory pass between the two sawn pieces of the offerings on Abraham's behalf. This is why the Abrahamic covenant is one of grace. It was based on God's promises, not Abraham's obedience. Another time we see the Shekinah is when God speaks to Moses from the burning bush (Exod. 3:2; Deut. 33:16), which leads into the story of Moses and the Shekinah's intervention to free the Israelites from Pharaoh's reign of slavery.

We know that when the Shekinah glory came down to Mount Sinai that it was a fearsome thing to behold. Exodus 19:16–19 describes the event:

> Then it came to pass on the third day, in the morning, that there were thunderings and lightnings, and a thick cloud on the mountain, and the sound of the trumpet was very loud; so that all the people who were in the camp trembled… Now Mount Sinai was completely in smoke, because the LORD descended upon it in fire. Its smoke ascended like the smoke of a furnace, and the whole mountain quaked greatly. And when the blast of the trumpet sounded long and became louder and louder, Moses spoke, and God answered him by voice.

Afterward, the people were so terrified they said to Moses, "You speak with us, and we will hear: but let not God speak with us, lest we die" (Exod. 20:19). Later, when the Shekinah presence of God descended and took up residence in the completed tabernacle, and later still, in the Temple, the glory of the LORD was so awesome and fearsome that the priests would be chased out, and they could not minister because of the cloud of the Shekinah's presence (1 Kings 8:10,11).

If the Shekinah glory was God's way to make His presence, His plans, and His desires manifest unto man, the zenith of that manifestation was when God made His glory to become flesh to literally shakan among us. Wasn't that the most intimate way for God to dwell with us and make Himself known to us, but to become one of us—to bridge the gulf between sinful humanity and a Holy God by becoming a fully man and fully God? Who could have imagined such a scenario? God the Father gave us God the Son, who gave up His life for us so that He could return to us His glory, God's Holy

Spirit. Jesus tells us, "But the Helper, the Holy Spirit, whom the Lord will send in My name, will teach you all things" (John 14:26). The Holy Spirit, who indwells us, teaches us, guides our steps, and leads us unto all wisdom and understanding. During this age, Shekinah fills the temple of our bodies with God's glory, but in the ages to come, She will fill the new temple in Jerusalem.

Modern Christians sometimes seem to clump God the Son and God's Shekinah glory into one entity, yet they are two distinct aspects of the Trinity. During this dispensation of grace, the Shekinah indwells all those who belong to Christ, but once Christians are called out during the rapture, the Shekinah still has a role to play during the end times. Old Testament prophets and early Christians looked forward to the return of the Shekinah.

In Israel's history, the glory of the Lord came and went a couple of times. She inhabited the first temple up until 568 BCE and then departed, as described in Ezekiel in chapter 11. Halfway through the tribulation, Jesus and the Shekinah will return, and it will not be a joyous event. During the millennium, Jesus will build a third temple and the Shekinah glory will return just how she left (Zechariah 2, Ezekiel 43). She will come down to the Mount of Olives and then enter the temple through the east gate (Ezek. 43:2–7).

Ezekiel saw both departures (from Solomon's temple and Ezekiel's temple) in two separate visions separated by a span of about ten years. He also vividly saw Shekinah's return with Christ during the tribulation, reiterated in Revelations 4 and 10, which takes place during the time of the Passover and marks the beginning of the second half of the great tribulation. This will be the most fearsome, terrifying event the world has ever known. Ezekiel explicitly describes this visitation of the glory of the Lord in his vision in chapter 1:

> The word of the Lord came expressly unto Ezekiel the priest...and the hand of the Lord was there upon him. And I looked, and behold, a whirlwind was coming out of the north, a great cloud

with raging fire engulfing itself; and brightness was all around it and radiating out of its midst like the color of amber, out of the midst of the fire. Also from within it came the likeness of four living creatures. And this was their appearance; they had the likeness of a man. Each one had four faces, and each one had four wings. Their legs were straight, and the sole of their feet were like the soles of calves' feet. They sparkled like the color of burnished bronze. The hands of a man were under their wings on their four sides; and each of the four had faces and wings. Their wings touched one another. The creatures did not turn when they went, but each one went straight forward.

As for the likeness of their faces, each had the face of a man; each of the four had the face of a lion on the right side, each of the four had the face of an ox on the left side, and each of the four had the face of an eagle. Thus were their faces…

As for the likeness of the living creatures, their appearance was like burning coals of fire, like the appearance of torches going back and forth among the living creatures. The fire was bright, and out of the fire went lightning. And the living creatures ran back and forth, in appearance like a flash of lightning.

Now as I looked at the living creatures, behold, a wheel was on the earth beside each living creature with its four faces. The appearance of the wheels and their workings was like the color of beryl, and all four had the same likeness. The appearance of their working was, as it were, a wheel in the middle of a wheel. When they moved, they went toward any one of four directions; they did not turn aside when they went. As for their rims, they were so high they were awesome; and their rims were full of eyes, all around the four of them. When the living creatures went, the wheels went beside them; and when the living creatures were lifted up from the earth, the wheels were lifted up. Wherever the spirit wanted to go, they went…

The likeness of the firmament above the heads of the living creatures was like the color of an awesome crystal, stretched out over their heads. And under the firmament their wings spread out straight, one toward another…A voice came from above the firmament that was over their heads; whenever they stood, they let down their wings.

And above the firmament over their heads was the likeness of a throne, in appearance like a sapphire stone; on the likeness of the throne was a likeness with the appearance of a man high above it. Also from the appearance of His waist and upward I saw, as it were, the color of amber with the appearance of fire all around within it; and from the appearance of His waist and downward I saw, as it were, the appearance of fire with brightness all around. Like the appearance of a rainbow in a cloud on a rainy day, so was the appearance of the brightness all around it. This was the appearance of the likeness of the glory of the Lord. (Ezekiel 1:3–28)

What is a woman's glory? Her hair is, right? Her hair is her glory because it is her covering (1 Cor. 11:15). In the same way, Shekinah is a covering, which is seen in the earthly realm as a dark fiery cloud (Exod. 24:16). The cloud by day protected the Israelites from the blistering desert sun, and the fiery cloud by night provided light and warmth. When Shekinah moved, the Israelites packed up their tents and followed. The Shekinah was their covering who dwelt with them to guide, shelter, and protect. Like a cloud, She does not have form, for She is spirit.

In the Old Testament, She covered, hovered, and temporarily rested on God's people. In the New Testament, She indwells God's people. Like water, She is mystical, miracle-like, hard to define, and impossible to pin down to the finite. During the great tribulation, She will become Ezekiel's vision in "real time." As the immense glory cloud descends over the temple during the middle of the tribulation, it will look to the world every bit like an alien invasion with cherubim creatures and gigantic-sized angels coming and going to and fro between the cloud and the Temple, unleashing on an unrepentant world horrific judgment and woe.

No man has ever been able to look into the Shekinah glory cloud to see what is going on from the inside. Man has only been able to see a dark cloud above his head or a fiery one; to see lightnings, fire, and smoke coming from it, and to hear thundering, loud noises like a rushing waterfalls and trumpets blaring. With just seeing and hearing this much, the Israelites were so terrified that they did not want to go anywhere near the glory cloud. In his vision, Ezekiel is allowed to see into the Shekinah cloud, and I believe he was reporting what the world will see when the Shekinah returns to the temple at the three-and-a-half-year mark of the tribulation. This event will be the ungodly man's worst nightmare, and the events that will follow will be even worse. Shekinah will be absolutely fearsome in all her glory, and fortunately for us, believers will not be there. We will already be with Christ in glory.

As we have said, Shekinah is spirit; She is a covering, a light, a radiance, and an essence of God, as well as a messenger who from time to time manifests God's plans and intentions to man. In this present age, She inhabits the hearts of God's people, because we are the temple of the Holy Spirit. To men, she usually appears as a light, and to nation of Israel, she appeared as a cloud. She is usually associated with the following:

She is associated with light:

- Genesis 1:2–3: "And the Spirit of God was hovering over the face of the waters. The God said, 'Let there be light'; and there was light."
- Ezekiel 43:2: "And, behold, the glory of the God of Israel came from the way of the east: and his voice was like a noise of many waters; and the earth shined with his glory."
- 1 Timothy 6:16: "He who is the blessed and only Potentate, the King of kings and Lord of lords, who alone has immortality, dwelling in unapproachable light [referring to the Ark of the Covenant], whom no man has seen or can see."

She is associated with the cherubim:

- Genesis 3:24: "So he drove out the man; and he placed at the east of the garden of Eden Cherubims, and a flaming sword which turned every way, to keep the way of the tree of life."
- Ezekiel 1:5–24; 10:1–5; 28:14: (Ezekiel describes the cherubim.)
- Revelation 4:6–8: "And before the throne there was a sea of glass like unto crystal: and round about the throne, were four beasts full of eyes before and behind. And the first beast was like a lion, and the second beast like a calf, and the third beast had a face as a man, and the fourth beast was like a flying eagle. And the four beasts had each of them

six wings about him; and they were full of eyes within; and they rest not day and night, saying, Holy, holy, holy, Lord God Almighty, which was, and is, and is to come."

She is associated with whirlwinds and clouds:

- Ezekiel 1:4: "And I looked, and behold a whirlwind came out of the north, a great cloud, and a fire enfolding itself, and a brightness was about it, and out of the midst thereof as the color of amber, out of the midst of the fire."
- Exodus 13:21–22: "And the Lord went before them by day in a pillar of a cloud, to lead them the way; and by night in a pillar of fire, to give them light; to go by day and night: He took not away the pillar of the cloud by day, nor the pillar of fire by night, from before the people."

She is associated with fire and hail:

- Exodus 24:17: "And the glory of the LORD was like a devouring fire on the top of the mount in the eyes of the children of Israel."
- Exodus 9:23, 24: "And fire ran along on the ground...and there was fire mingled with hail."

She is associated with covering:

- Exodus 14:19: "And the Angel of God, who went before the camp of Israel, moved and went behind them; and the pillar of cloud went from before them and stood behind them."
- Exodus 14:24, 25: "The LORD looked down upon the army of the Egyptians through the pillar of fire and cloud, and He troubled the army of the Egyptians. And He took off their chariot wheels, so they drove them with difficulty,

and the Egyptians said, "Lets us flee from the face of Israel, for the LORD fights for them against the Egyptians."

She is associated with fiery horses and chariots:

- 2 Kings 2:11: "Behold, there appeared a chariot of fire, and horses of fire, and parted them both asunder; and Elijah went up by a whirlwind into heaven."

All the symbolism associated with the Shekinah would strike fear in most people. Yet, to look into the Shekinah cloud will be the most fearsome of all. We are so very blessed that we will never experience the kind of wrath that will be unleashed on Satan, the antichrist, and all those who follow him. Jesus took God's wrath for our sins in His own body so that God will never be angry with us again. We are His bride, His beloved, and we are fearsome in His power and righteousness. We are His shekinahs during this age, but in the ages to come, all you can say is that Shekinah will be a fearsome thing to behold.

During the millennium, both Jesus and the Shekinah are returning—Jesus to rule and reign as King of king and Lord of lords, and the Shekinah to support Him in all Her fearsome glory. We, the bride of Christ, also come back with Jesus to reign and rule with Him for one thousand years. At the end of the thousand years, Satan is given one last chance to lead a revolt, but it is quickly squelched, and then Satan and all his cohorts will be thrown into the lake of fire. Then Jesus creates a new heaven and a new earth.

As I read Revelation 21:22–27, it seems perfectly clear that in the new heaven and new earth that both the glory of the Lord and the Lamb of God are the new temple in the new Jerusalem, as well as its light source. In verse 22 and 23, it says,

> And I saw no temple therein: for the Lord God Almighty and the Lamb are the temple of it. And

the city had no need of the sun, neither of the moon, to shine in it: for the glory of God did lighten it, and the Lamb is the light thereof.

The glory of God *and* the Lamb of God are the light for the new heavenly city. Two entities, two sources of light, yet both, equal manifestations of His glorious radiance, His ineffable Spirit, and His unfathomable love.

As a Christian, I have never doubted that Jesus will be the new temple and the light of it, but I never noticed or understood that His Shekinah glory will have a vital role to play by His side. The Shekinah Glory is going to return with Jesus in the end times. During this church age, Shekinah's radiance resides in every believer. She is the resurrection life and power of Jesus that indwells us. She is our Comforter, our Helper, our Healer, our Divine Covering and Protection. She fills our temple with the glory of God. All power and authority that Jesus had while He walked on this earth is now imparted to us. When She alighted upon Jesus in the form of a dove, God the Father said, "This is my beloved Son, in whom I am well pleased" (Matt. 3:17).

When we invited Jesus into our hearts, the Holy Spirit, His Shekinah glory, entered our hearts and all the angels in Heaven proclaimed, "This is my beloved daughter, in whom I am well pleased." From the moment we received Jesus into our hearts, our Shekinah glory has been directing our steps, comforting our hurts, healing our bodies, protecting our loved ones, and gracing our lives with the beauty of the Son. She reveals our Heavenly Father's heart toward us, that He loves each and every one of us intimately and infinitely beyond what we could think or imagine. She directs our thoughts toward Jesus, who is our wisdom, our righteousness, and our Savior. Just as the Israelites experienced the protection, presence, and power of the Shekinah glory of the Lord during their wilderness testing, so too She covers us with Her protecting presence and power during our times of trials and tribulations as the power of Christ indwells us.

Throughout the history of man, we see God's desire to dwell with, to shakan with us. We see God's heart is to gather to Himself a people the way a mother hen gathers her chicks beneath her wings. His story toward us is one of indefatigable and immeasurable love. Although we are stubborn, stiff-necked, willful, and rebellious, He still loves us. Like an ardent lover, He wooed us and relentlessly pursued us, eventually sending His own beloved Son to die for us, so that we might be redeemed. His Precious Son paid our bail, gave us a "get out of hell free" card, and paid our ransom with His own holy, sinless blood. Jesus laid down His life for us while we were cursing and spitting on Him and beating Him until His bones were flayed open. Some may lay down their life for a good man, but who lays down their life for those who despise Him? The answer is, God does, and He did. He sent His Son into the world to lay down His life for each one of us; for those who love Him, and even for those who don't. That is how much our Heavenly Father desires to dwell with us.

His dearest desire is that none should perish, but that all would come to Him and receive eternal life through His Precious Son. God the Father manifested His great love toward us, in that while we were yet sinners, Christ died for us. Now, we love Him because He first loved us. When we ask Jesus into our heart, His Shekinah glory takes up residence and shakans within us, and we become the temple of the Holy Spirit. His glorious radiance fills us so that our countenance literally shines with His divine health, love, and joy. We are gloriously adored, greatly favored, and abundantly blessed. We are His beloved shekinahs! As Christian women across this planet begin to walk in the full identity of who we are as His glorious shekinahs, as we unite as one force for healing, comfort, and His shalom peace, truly, it will be a fearsome thing to behold!

Revelation

Once I felt powerless and insignificant, but now I know I am His beloved shekinah, and I am fearsome in His glory and majesty.

Prayer of Praise

Lord, thank You that You created me a force to be reckoned with. When I think of the load I have been called to bear, as in giving birth; raising children; juggling the demands of husband, children, and career; as well as often singlehandedly managing the business of the home, as in shopping, meal planning, cooking, laundry, cleaning, and shuttling the children to all their events; truly, I am a wonder woman. Thank You, Lord, for providing me with all the energy and talents that I need to manage life. Your goodness toward me is startling and so appreciated.

Through the centuries, women have often been called to carry the greater load, and You have given us the strength to do so. Thank You for gracing me with the ability to meet the needs of my husband, my children, my friends, as well as to meet all my other obligations with work and church. Thank You, Lord, that You fill me with Your resurrection life and power, You grace me with Your glory and beauty, and You created me mighty, "undevourable," and victorious in Your strength and majesty. In You I can do all things, and with You, all things are possible. No dream is too big, no aspiration too high, for You are my great and mighty God, and with You, sweet Jesus, I am Your fearsome shekinah and there is no limit to what I can accomplish.

Arise, O Shekinah, You Glorious, Beautiful She

Notice, again, Genesis 1:26–27, "And God said, 'Let *us* make man in *our* image, after *our* likeness…So God created man in his *own* image, in the image of God He created him; male and female He created them" (emphasis mine). Before the foundations of the world, God had planned to create male and female in "Our" image. Notice the "us" and the "our". Who are the "us" and the "our"? Father, Son, and the Holy Spirit, right? Verse 27 leaves no doubt that man was made in the image of God, and we know that Jesus is His Son, so who does that leave for the female to have been modeled after? The only other "us" or "our" not represented in human form in these verses is the Holy Spirit.

Professor R. P. Nettlehorst, an author and theologian who holds a Ph.D. in Semantic languages, uncovered evidence for a feminine Holy Spirit while working on his doctoral dissertation. In an article he wrote entitled, *More Than Just a Controversy: All about the Holy Spirit*, he asks, "Is there a question about the gender of the Holy Spirit?" He gives his answer in the following story:

> In my graduate Semitics program at UCLA, one of the languages I had to study was Syriac, a dialect of Aramaic written with rounded letters reminiscent of modern Arabic. Syriac was the language of people in northern Mesopotamia, from at least 300 BC until the time Arabic became dominant in the region, around 1000 AD. Most

of the Syriac documents available today were produced by a Monophysite branch of Christianity, today known as the Syrian Orthodox Church. One striking puzzlement of the texts, at least to me, was the constant reference to the Holy Spirit as "she". I was aware, of course, that in Aramaic (and hence in the dialect know as Syriac) the natural gender of the word "spirit" was feminine.

An example of Syriac theology is found in the apocryphal Acts of Thomas; it is usually assumed that this particular work was influenced by speculative gnostic Judaism because it contains the notion, that associated with God was a wisdom, or creative power—a spirit—which was feminine (Acts of Thomas 5:50).

Spring 1986

I was teaching advanced Hebrew, and I had decided to take the class through the book of Judges. As we read along, I noticed something odd about Judges 3:10:

"The Spirit of Yahweh came upon Caleb's younger brother…"

In English, this passage from Judges doesn't appear startling, but in Hebrew something strange leapt out at me; "came upon" was a third person FEMININE verb, indicating it's subject "Spirit" was being understood as a feminine noun. Hebrew is not like Aramaic in its use of the word "spirit". While the word is exclusively feminine in Aramaic, in Hebrew it is sometimes masculine. Therefore, the question that came to mind was why had the author of Judges chosen here to make the Spirit of Yahweh feminine, when he could just as easily have made it masculine?

I just shrugged my shoulders and went on, not overly concerned. Occasionally, I thought, one finds something inexplicable in the Bible: no big deal. But then came Judges 6:34. Again, "Spirit of Yahweh" was feminine. At this point I decided to consult the concordance. Much to my surprise, every occurrence of "Spirit of Yahweh" in Judges is feminine. As I pondered that, I recalled Genesis 1:2, the first occurrence of "Spirit of Yahweh" in the Bible, and realized to my shock that it too is feminine.

Back to the concordance. Out of 84 OT uses of the word "spirit", in contexts traditionally assumed to be references to the Holy Spirit, 75 times it is either explicitly feminine or indeterminable (due to lack of verb or adjective). Only nine times can "spirit" be construed as masculine, and in those cases it is unclear that it is a reference to God's Holy Spirit anyway.

The New Testament references to the Holy Spirit are not helpful for conclusively deciding on the gender of the Holy Spirit, since "spirit" in Greek is neuter, and so is referred to as "it" by the New Testament writers.

The conclusion of all this is that our traditional assumption of a masculine Spirit is questionable; in fact, the evidence seems overwhelming that the Spirit should be viewed as "She", which does seem to make sense, since the other two members of the Godhead are labeled "Father" and "Son". (p. 3-5)

According to Professor Nettlehorst, in the Eastern Orthodox religions it has always been common knowledge that the Holy Spirit is feminine, but when the Roman Catholic Church split during the East-West Schism in 1054, that knowledge got lost in semantics. Through dedicated theologians, God is bringing to light the truth of women's identity in the Godhead; that we are made in the image of the Holy Spirit and She is a "Beautiful Glorious She". How thrilling to see my revelation confirmed, to see this historically obscured truth surface and come to light through the ancient texts! It just makes sense that the Third Person of the Trinity is feminine.

In all of creation, God loves trinity. Father, Son, and Holy Spirit; Jesus, man, and woman; the marriage covenant (Jesus, husband, and wife); body, soul, and spirit; mental, emotional, and physical; water molecule (oxygen, hydrogen, and hydrogen); sky, earth, and water; the three states of matter (solid, liquid, gas), three gifts of the wise men, three arks, and the list goes on and on. The Trinity of the Godhead is represented in the rays of the sun. Heat rays you can feel but not see, light rays you can see but not feel, and actinic rays, which you can neither see nor feel. The Holy Spirit you can feel but not see; Jesus you can see but not feel; and God the Father, whom no man has seen nor can feel. God loves trinity because He is a Trinity.

A water molecule is a unique trinity. Water is actually a miracle-like substance that has many physical properties that it shouldn't have, according to what we understand about chemistry and physics. Robert Laing states that water has at least twenty-one anomalies that defy the laws of chemistry and physics, but without even one of these anomalies, there would not be life as we know it on our planet. These mystical, godlike properties give new meaning to the verse, "The Spirit of God moved upon the face of the waters" (Gen. 1:2). Water is so complex, hard to explain, and yet essential to life, isn't it interesting that Jesus referred to the Holy Spirit as "living water"?

One fascinating anomaly is that water expands when frozen, whereas most substances contract. If water did not expand and get lighter as it freezes, ice would sink and freeze oceans, rivers, and lakes from the bottom up, killing everything underneath it. Because God made water to expand as it freezes, it floats, creating a blanket of insulation for life below it. Water also contracts at 40 degrees Fahrenheit, becoming more dense, which causes spring and fall turnover of lakes in temperate climates. In tropical climates, where the water is warmer, hurricanes, typhoons, monsoons, and torrential rain replaces spring and fall turnover. Because warm water is less dense than cold water, it floats on top, insulating the waters below. Water also has inexplicably high melting and boiling points compared to other substances. If water acted like the other substances that are close to it on the Periodic Table, all water on our planet would be in the gaseous state and there would be no life on earth.

How like God to use a miracle life-giving substance like water, which man cannot fully explain, to describe His Holy Spirit. Jesus said, "Most assuredly I say to you, unless one is born of water and the Spirit, he cannot enter the kingdom of God" (John 3:5). Jesus told the Samaritan woman at Jacob's well, "Whoever drinks of this water will thirst again, but whoever drinks of the water that I shall give him will never thirst. But the water I shall give him will become in him a fountain of water springing up into everlasting life" (John 4:13–14). On the last day of the Feast of Tabernacles, Jesus stood and cried out,

> If anyone thirsts, let him come to Me and drink.
> He who believes in Me, as Scripture has said, out
> of his heart will flow rivers of living water. But
> this He spoke concerning the Spirit, whom those

believing in him would receive; for the Holy Spirit was not yet given, because Jesus was not yet glorified. (John 7:37–39)

And being assembled together with them, He commanded them not to depart from Jerusalem, but to wait for the Promise of the Father, which He said, "You have heard from Me; for John truly baptized with water, but you not many days from now…you shall receive power when the Holy Spirit has come upon you; and you shall be witnesses to Me in Jerusalem, and in all Judea and Samaria, and to the end of the earth." (Acts 1:4–8)

There is no question that the Holy Spirit is likened unto water. The two words are used interchangeably. It is mind-boggling to think that God's feminine, ineffable essence is likened unto God's miracle, life-giving substance of water. The first mention of "life" in the Bible is the verse "Let the waters bring forth life abundantly," telling us that life came forth from water, much like the way babies are brought forth from water (Gen. 1:20). Water is the essence of physical life on our planet, the way the Holy Spirit is the essence of spiritual life.

The picture of a water molecule is a perfect picture of the Trinity because neither Jesus nor the Holy Spirit glorifies themselves; they only glorify God the Father. Jesus and the Holy Spirit have different but equal parts to play in supporting the Godhead, in the same way men and women have different but equal parts to play as children of God. Men and women have been given dominion over all the earth. We are called to be God's representatives and witnesses on the planet and to co-reign with Jesus as His king-priests and queen-priestesses. In like manner, in the new heaven and the new earth, Jesus and His Shekinah glory will coreign, as well as provide the light source for the New Temple.

I have heard many men comment that, like water, women are rather mystical, unexplainable, and unknowable. We can draw many analogies as to how women are like water. Water has an unusual ability to dissolve other substances, the way women have an extraordinary ability to dissolve conflict and strife. We are by design peacemakers, and most of us are very adept at calming and soothing the waters. Water molecules can easily form bonds with other molecules in the same way that women are highly relational and can easily form bonds with others. Water flows the same way that women are typically pretty good at rolling with the flow. As comforters/helpers we are well-designed to bend, flow, and adapt to the needs of others, especially to our husbands.

Water has an unusually high boiling and melting point, in the same way, women are generally much slower to anger and rage than men, and we are quicker to thaw and to make amends. Water has a high specific heat compared to other materials, which means it takes a lot more heat to raise its temperature. In the same way, it generally takes more heat to raise a woman's temper than a man's, who are by nature more volatile and easier to provoke to wrath. Lastly, water has the unique ability to pass through cell membranes and climb to great heights in plants and trees through osmosis and capillary force. This same mysterious action takes place on a microscopic level within the bodies of all living creatures. In the same way, women have the uncanny ability to penetrate the hearts and minds of their loved ones with her faith, confidence, and love, and to inspire them to rise to great heights. We have all heard the expression, "Behind every great man is a great woman."

Water speaks of physical birth, of spiritual birth, of regeneration, of purification, of the word of God, and of the Holy Spirit. In the new heaven and the new earth, living waters flow out from the throne of God, in the same way that, today, it flows out from us as seven-fold blessings because we are His temples on earth. The "living water of the Word," the Holy Spirit, is being poured out on God's people as a torrential flood of blessing. In Revelation 5:11–12 it says, "Then I looked, and I heard the voice of many angels around the throne, the living creatures, and the elders...saying, 'Worthy is the Lamb who was slain to receive *power* and *riches* and *wisdom* and *strength* and *honor* and *glory* and *blessing!*'" (emphasis mine.) As His glorious shekinahs and blood-bought heirs of the Most High God in Christ Jesus, our Rock of Salvation has been smitten, and gushing rivers of living water are flooding our lives with seven-fold blessings straight from the throne room of God.

In Hosea 12:10, we are told, "I have also spoken by the prophets, and I have multiplied visions, and used similitudes, by the ministry of the prophets." Similitudes are like parables and faith pictures; they make comparisons using something similar that is familiar and known. The Bible is filled with many similitudes, types, and shadows. In the word *rib*, which is a word strongly connected to the creation of women, several similitudes can be found. Looking at 1 Kings 6:8, the high priest went once a year with the blood through the right side of the house of the Lord and up the winding staircase into the Holy of Holies where Shekinah dwelt. In Exodus 26 and Ezekiel 41, the word for *side*, when used in reference to the tabernacle or the temple is "rib." This verse tells us that the high priest went in and out of the temple through the right rib. Four times the Bible uses the phrase "spear smote him under the fifth rib." Four is the number of creation, and five is the number of grace.

When Jesus hung on the cross, a Roman soldier pierced his ribs, probably under the fifth one, and from His wound blood and water flowed out on the ground. Jesus's saving blood was poured out "under the rib of grace" for the sins of the world, "His creation," and the water of the Word, the Holy Spirit, poured forth, birthing the church. When Ezekiel is describing the glory of the Lord, he recorded, "Now the Cherubim stood on the right side (rib) of the house (Temple), when the man (Jesus) went in; and the cloud filled the inner court" (Ezek. 10:3). Since the earthly temple mirrors the heavenly temple, I wonder if this could be a picture telling us that before the beginning of time, Jesus and the

Holy Spirit were birthed in the same way from the right side of God under the fifth rib? Or is this how they come and go from His presence? Just curious.

Another rib similitude is that when God refers to the "side of the ark" and the "side of the altar of burnt offering" (the holiest objects in the Tabernacle), the word He uses for *side* is "rib." (Exod. 37:3–4; 38:7). In both cases, the priests were required to carry the ark (or the altar) by placing staves through four rings on the sides of them. A stave is a wooden pole or spear. The rings mean "to sink into" as in a signet ring sunk into wax, the ark is a picture of our redemption, and the altar of burnt offering represents God exhausting His wrath for the sins of the world in the body of His Son. This is a similitude that prophesied, a wooden spear would be sunk into the rib of Christ, our Divine Redeemer, and that Jesus would be pierced for our transgressions and burnt as our sacrificial Lamb of God. Isaiah 53 prophesied that Jesus would be pierced, stricken, bruised, and His body brutally marred more than any man, yet the Bible said it pleased God to bring His Son to such grief, because by doing so, many would be saved. What unimaginable, glorious love—that God offered His own beloved Son for the sins of the world, so that by one man's sacrifice, many might be saved!

Another interesting rib analogy is that chromosomes are shaped like a rib. God created man with an X chromosome and a Y. When God took a rib from Adam's side to fashion us, perhaps He took an X chromosome (a rib) from Adam's rib, then added another X chromosome to create a woman. However it happened, there is no disputing that men have one X chromosome, which is the female chromosome. In other words, half our chromosomes came from man, meaning we are half of man and he is half of us. The Bible tells us, "So husbands ought to love their wives as their own bodies; he who loves his wife loves himself. For no one ever hated their own flesh, but nourishes and cherishes it, just as the Lord does the church" (Eph. 5:28–29).

When a man hates or demeans a woman, he sins against his own flesh. Woman came out of man, we share half his DNA, because it was God's design that we should be loved, adored, and respected in the same way that man loves, adores and respects himself. By taking us from a place near to man's heart, God meant for us to be cherished, treasured, and treated gently, as tenderly as man cares for his own heart. This is why God told man to love his wife as he loves his own body.

So many types and shadows point to woman as being an extra special creation; holy, even. We were fashioned from a living, breathing being and then formed by the hand of God. God called us comforter/helpers, the same word he uses for the Holy Spirit. This is not insignificant. He is telling us that we were part of the Godhead from the beginning, part of the total essence of the Godhead. We represent the softer, relational side of God. We are the nurturers, the comforters, the healers, the peacemakers, and the tenderness seen in the world.

It would be such a harsh, cruel existence if it were not for the grace and beauty supplied by His glorious shekinahs. We are the reason that windows have curtains, beds have dust ruffles, tables have placemats, houses have gardens, children have teachers, hospitals have nurses, cities have soup kitchens, neighbors have dinner parties, families have someone who cares for them when they are sick, friends can find an empathetic ear, and on and on. Like the Holy Spirit, we are the force for comfort, help, healing, and love on our planet, like living water poured out upon dry ground.

There have been several Christian ages in times past when women were honored, cherished, and treated with gentle consideration as the weaker, more tender-hearted vessel. We are physically weaker than men and less able to endure some of life's harsher or meaner aspects, and not so long ago, women were protected by godly men from having to deal with the baser things of life. Throughout the history of the Bible, God the Father elevates women to a noble status, which He made manifest when He entrusted woman to carry and nurture His Son, as well as specifically mentioning several women in the genealogy of Christ. Jesus elevates women in His ministry, relying on our help for emotional and financial support. While God gave us a different skill set of strengths than men, it is our gifts that complete man and perfect His Trinity. Godly men recognize that women are the other half of themselves—the part that brings harmony, balance, completeness, and sensitivity into their lives. Godly men live with women in an understanding way, giving glory to the woman as the weaker vessel physically, yet the stronger vessel relationally and spiritually, and in doing so, God hears and honors their prayers.

God has told us through His word that men and women share equal parts in the Godhead and His Trinity; that both male and female are made in His image, and that we were both designed to glorify God and to complement one another with our strengths and talents. Together we create a three-fold cord that cannot be easily broken. When we give honor to one another's strengths as vital to the function of the Trinity, God richly blesses the marriage covenant. Women are called to submit to their husband's leadership and to support him in every way possible, and men are called to love their wives as Christ loves the church, giving honor to her as heirs of Grace. As husbands and wives love as Christ loves, their union is spiritually, physically, and emotionally blessed.

When men malign, demean, and abuse women, they cannot not expect to receive blessings from God. With their words and actions, they destroy their own flesh—they sin against their own bodies. The desire to deal harshly and callously with women comes straight from the pit of hell. It is Satan's agenda to attack, abuse, and destroy women and her children, and this mind-set has no part in the hearts of godly men.

As Christian women, we must take responsibility for not allowing or tolerating this mind-set. We must teach our husbands, our children, our churches, and ourselves, God's view of women and restore ourselves to our true position in the Godhead, in our churches, and in our families. We must arise, O shekinahs, and take our rightful position as His comforters, helpers, healers, and as His representatives of living waters poured out upon this planet.

We were especially fashioned by God and modeled after the Holy Spirit. We are His glorious shekinahs and it is time for each one of us to rise up and to walk in the fullness of who we are in the Godhead. He says to us, "You are fair, my love, and there is no spot in you" (Song of Sol. 4:7). He tells us, "Eye has not seen, nor ear heard, nor have entered into the heart of man the things which God has prepared for those who love Him" (1 Cor. 2:9). Jesus said,

> I do not pray for these alone, but also for those who will believe in Me through their word; that they all may be one, as You, Father, are in Me and I in You; that they also may be one in Us, that the world may believe that You sent Me. And the glory which You gave Me I have given them, that they may be one just as We are one: I in them, and You in Me; that they may be made perfect in one, and that the world may know that You have sent Me, and have loved them as You have loved Me. (John 17:20–23)

God's glory has been restored to us. He tells us that in Christ we are crowned with His glory, honor, power, wisdom, riches, strength, and blessing (Ps. 8:5, Rev 5:11–12, 1 John 4:17). When the Holy Spirit came down at Pentecost, God's glory was restored, and even better, instead of just resting on us as in Old Testament times, now the Holy Spirit takes up residence inside us. She indwells and shakans with us, and we receive power when the Holy Spirit takes up residence in us.

As His shekinahs, as temples of the Glory of God, He has given us a superabundant life of so much more. In Romans 5:17, He tells us, "For if by the one man's offense death reigned through the one, *much more* those who receive *abundance of grace* and of *the gift of righteousness* will reign in life through the One, Jesus Christ" (emphasis mine). When God created us, He did not intend for us to grow old or to become sick and die. He did not intend for us to be poor, weak, or powerless. These are all part of the curse. When Christ died, He won our victory over death, disease, and the curse, giving us an abundance of His grace, as well as His gift of righteousness, so that we may reign in life. The more we believe in His superabundant, unearned, undeserved, unmerited favor, the more we know that we have been made righteous through the precious blood of Jesus, the more we will reign over all forms of sickness and disease. The more we believe in His grace, the more we reign over every manner of the curse.

Every good and perfect gift is already ours. Every blessing is already ours. We are heirs to our Abraham blessing and Sarah blessing, all in Benjamin-generation-blessing proportions. This means we get five times the financial blessing and the renewal of our health, youth, and beauty than the Old Testament saints. We can expect divine favor and preferential treatment because of who we are in Christ, and because His Shekinah glory resides in us. So arise and shine, O beautiful shekinahs! Glory and revel in your role in the Godhead! Walk into the fullness of who God designed you to be, and apprehend your rightful position as His shekinahs, knowing that you are deeply loved, highly favored, and greatly blessed! Lift up your hands in praise and proclaim, "Thank you, Jesus, that I am made in the image of Your Holy Spirit, that I am Your comforter and helper and glorious radiance on the planet." Sing unto the Lord:

> Arise and shine; for my light has come! Arise and shine for my light has come!
>> And the glory of the Lord is risen upon me; arise and shine!
>> Behold, the darkness shall cover the earth, and deep darkness shall cover the people;
>> But the Lord will arise over me; His glory will be seen upon me.

The world will come to my light, and kings to the brightness of my rising.

Lift up my eyes all around and see; they all gather around to come to me.

My sons shall come from afar; my daughter shall be nursed at my side.

Then I shall see and become radiant; my heart shall swell with joy;

Because the abundance of the universe is turned to me,

And the wealth of the world shall come to me.

So arise and shine; for my light is come! Arise and shine; for my light is come!

And the glory of the Lord is risen upon me; arise and shine! (Isa. 60:1–5)

The glory of the Lord is upon you; She indwells you; She goes before you; She follows after you; She surrounds you like a shield; She emanates from you as divine radiance; She infuses your heart with joy and gladness; and She draws every blessing of God toward you. You are irreversibly loved and irrevocably blessed! So arise and shine, O shekinah; you beautiful glorious she!

Revelation

Once I believed as a woman that I didn't matter much to God, but now I know that I am His precious shekinah, that I was modeled after the Holy Spirit, and that I was part of the plan and part of the Godhead from the beginning.

Prayer of Praise

Thank You, Jesus, for revealing to me the full identity of who I am in You, Lord. You call me a daughter of Sarah because I am Your heavenly princess. You call me the seed of Abraham through faith, a blood-bought heir of the Most High. You call me a queen-priestess, and where the word of a queen is, there is power, and as the word of a priestess is, so shall it be done. You call me a comforter and helper, the same word you use for the Holy Spirit. Everything about me is made in the image of things above. I reflect the feminine heart of God, and I was part of the creation plan from the beginning.

You created me special from a living, breathing created being. Every other living creature was created from dirt, but not me. You fashioned me from Your glorious creation, man, and then You formed me. I did not come from baser substances, I came from things above, and I am the pinnacle of Your creation.

You created me to be a comforter, a helper, a healer, and a covering for my family and the world. Give me, O lord, all Your ministering gifts so that I can manifest the fullest measure of all that I am in You. Fill me from the atomic level outward with Your glory, beauty, and grace so that I may walk in the divine manifestations of my destiny as Your precious shekinah.

> Lord, make
> Your face to shine upon me,
> Your radiance to fill me,
> Your Spirit to infuse me,
> Your glory to cover me,
> Your Shekinah to indwell me,
> Your Comforter to heal me
> Your Helper to direct me,
> Till I am wholly anointed—
> A beautiful glorious she.

References

Nettlehorst, R. P. *More Than Just a Controversy: All About the Holy Spirit*. Quartz Hill School of Theology.
Accessed November 22, 2017. http://www.theology.edu/journal/volume3/spirit.htm.

Keyser, John D. *Yehovah's Shekinah Glory*. Hope of Israel Ministries. Accessed September 15, 2016. http://www.hope-of-israel.org/glory.htm.

Miller, Fred P. *Zechariah and Jewish Renewal: From Gloom to Glory*. Clermont, Florida: Moellerhaus Publishing, 1992

New King James Bible, Holman Bible Publishers, 2013.

Peterson, Eugene H. *The Message: The Bible in Contemporary Language*. Colorado Springs, CO: NavPress Publishing Group, 2005.

Prince, Joseph. *The Benjamin Generation*. Joseph Prince Teaching Resources. 2006.

Prince, Joseph. *Destined to Reign Devotional*. Tulsa, Oklahoma: Harrison House, Inc., 2008.

Thayer, Joseph H. *Thayer's Greek-English Lexicon of the New Testament*. Peabody, MA: Hendrickson Publishers Marketing, LLC, 2015.

Strong, James. *The New Strong's Expanded Exhaustive Concordance of the Bible*. Nashville, TN: Thomas Nelson Publishers, 2010.

About the Author

Eulalie Hendricks is an educator, author, wife, mother of three, and grandmother of eight. Most of her teaching career was spent in a one-room schoolhouse in North Pole, Alaska, where she had the blessed privilege of homeschooling her own children through the grades. She also served many years as a children's minister and children's music minister. Presently, she lives in Portland, Oregon, and works for an international business couple as a private tutor. Her dearest desire is to move into full-time women's ministry, offering seminars and workshops, leading women into the truth of who they are in the eyes of God, teaching them how to apprehend and walk in the fullness of all that is theirs in Christ Jesus, opening Scripture in such a way that it sets their hearts aflame with His hope, His glory, and His power, and revealing who they really are—*a beautiful, glorious she.*

CPSIA information can be obtained
at www.ICGtesting.com
Printed in the USA
FFHW021147170219
50561259-55882FF